Crest-back Boston rocker, circa 1832. *See Pattern 7.* Marked, Hitchcock Alford and Co.
Courtesy Index of American Design, National Gallery of Art, Washington, D. C.

HOW TO RESTORE
AND DECORATE CHAIRS
IN EARLY AMERICAN STYLES

by Roberta Ray Blanchard

DOVER PUBLICATIONS, INC.
NEW YORK

Published in Canada by General Publishing Company, Ltd., 30
Lesmill Road, Don Mills, Toronto, Ontario.
Published in the United Kingdom by Constable and Company, Ltd.,
10 Orange Street, London WC2H 7EG.

This Dover edition, first published in 1981, is an unabridged repub-
lication of the work originally published in 1952 by M. Barrows and Co.,
Inc., N.Y., with the title *How to Restore and Decorate Chairs*.

International Standard Book Number: 0-486-24177-7
Library of Congress Catalog Card Number: 81-67444

Manufactured in the United States of America
Dover Publications, Inc.
180 Varick Street
New York, N.Y. 10014

For
ROBBIE,
JOAN,
and
SALLY

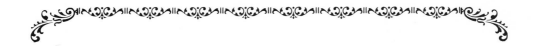

Contents

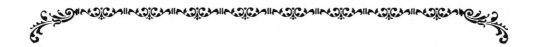

Illustrations

Acknowledgments

THE IDEA of assembling a book of authentic chair stencils and brush-stroke patterns for amateur decorators came to me after I had received many letters and requests for information from all over the United States. Men, in particular, the husbands of the veritable army of ladies who have lately become interested in tray-painting and bronze stenciling, have been asking for a book on restoring and decorating old chairs, and they have been quick to see the possibilities of employing these Early American craft-techniques on various pieces of furniture.

A half dozen mismatched chairs may be related in a short time by a coat of black paint and the application of a simple gold-powder stencil. Because a beginner who has no skill in drawing may trace and cut out a stencil and use it to obtain rather spectacular results, the craft of bronze stenciling has been revitalized. It is a simple matter to apply these antique stencils, for the bronze powders are rubbed over the pattern with the finger-tip instead of a brush. The stencil may be used over and over again, and in this way the decorator is provided with a tool by which he may put an identical pattern on several chairs. Freehand brush-stroke paint-

ing, the other Early American technique, is not quite so easy to do, but by following the step-by-step directions in this book, I believe anyone may restore life and glow to partially-obliterated decorations or create new patterns in the authentic style of nineteenth-century painted furniture.

I am grateful to the many organizations and individuals who have generously allowed photographs to be taken of cherished antiques in their collections. My thanks are also due to The Metropolitan Museum of Art, New York; The Philadelphia Museum of Art; The Society for the Preservation of New England Antiquities, Boston; Index of American Design in the National Gallery in Washington; The Museum of Fine Arts, Boston; The Museum of the City of New York; The Hitchcock Chair Company, Riverton, Connecticut; Essex Institute, Salem, Massachusetts; Winchester Public Library; and also to Mr. George Murray, Mr. Morton Bartlett, Miss Corinne Meade, Miss Amelia McSwiggan, Miss Esther Oldham, and to many friends and antique dealers who have answered questions and loaned their chairs for color sketches and measurements.

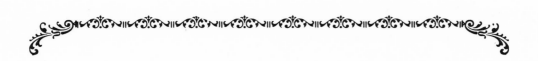

FOREWORD: IT'S FUN TO DECORATE CHAIRS

HAVE YOU ever wished that you could refinish an antique chair? Have you ever stumbled on an old "Hitchcock" in your mother's attic and longed for the artistic ability to replace the worn gilt decoration on its wide back slat? Have you ever seen a sturdy but dilapidated "arrow-back" or "fiddle-back" at an auction and wished that you were clever enough to restore it to original beauty? If you have, this is your book.

You need not be especially artistic to follow these easy directions. Removing cracked and worn paint, filling up holes, and repainting a chair can become a fascinating project for men as well as women. A very little skill in tracing a full-scale pattern from this book will put you on the way to redecorating your chair, and a small amount of patience in varnishing and rubbing down will complete your work and remake your battered relic into a beautiful piece of furniture once more.

If it is a new "unfinished" chair that has captured your imagination or if your husband would like to puzzle out the directions and put together one of the "knocked-down" models that are being widely advertised today, you will find instructions here for decorating a new chair as well as an old one. And if you do not like painted furniture, there are workable rules for varnishing and rubbing down old or new chairs with no decoration on them at all. Refinishing furniture is fun. Anyone can do it, and the results are most rewarding.

I have included patterns for many different sizes and shapes of chairs in order that you may adapt them to your own heirlooms or reproductions. Even the simple Victorian bedroom chairs, one or two of which linger still in almost everyone's house, are worth decorating. They can be freshened with paint and patterns to become a bright accent at a desk or in dining room or foyer. There is great satisfaction in bringing back a faded old design or in creating a new one.

Before actually starting your project, look at the photographs in this book. Find the chair that looks most like the one you plan to work on. Read carefully the section which describes this chair. Decide after examining photographs and reading the text whether stenciling or freehand painting was used in applying the old decoration. Then refer to the various chapter divisions for the particular process used on your chair. It is here that step-by-step instructions are given.

Have all the necessary materials at hand before you begin to work. If you are a beginner in stenciling or brush-stroke painting, do not attempt to decorate your chair until you have first tried out the pattern on practice paper. It is very helpful to work out the design on black paper so that you can become familiar with the component parts of the pattern before working on your final project. It should be an exciting and pleasant experience to paint your first chair and my good wishes go with you in your initial attempt at furniture decoration.

ROBERTA RAY BLANCHARD

May, 1952
Winchester, Massachusetts

PART I

Methods and Techniques

1

Types of Decoration

THERE ARE two methods of placing designs on painted furniture: stenciling with bronze powders on tacky varnish, and freehand or brush-stroke painting.

BRONZE STENCILING

Bronze stenciling was popularized in the early days of the nineteenth century when Lambert Hitchcock manufactured great quantities of decorated chairs in his Connecticut factory. Although most stenciled chairs remaining today are "Hitchcocks," the type of decoration did not originate in the busy little factory at Hitchcocksville. Stenciling on furniture with metallic powders or "bronze stenciling" was an outgrowth of the freehand bronze painting used on American-made Empire furniture. Much of this was produced by cabinetmakers in New York and Philadelphia. These craftsmen admired the brass insets and costly filigree of the imported French furniture of the period with its elaborate, super-imposed decoration on Napoleonic bureaus, consoles, and sofas.

American cabinetmakers substituted for the ex-pensive metal inlays clever brushwork in bronze powders and gold leaf. Excellent examples of the early pieces may be seen in The Museum of the City of New York. The workmanship is fine and there are occasional examples of stenciling in conjunction with brush-stroke painting. As business expanded and more orders came than could be executed by the slow painstaking bronze-painting process, more and more short-cuts were taken by means of stencils, and it is interesting to trace the growth of stenciling from this point.

BRUSH-STROKE PAINTING

Quite different from bronze painting and stenciling was the freehand decoration on earlier painted furniture of the English cabinetmakers, Sheraton and Hepplewhite. Their chairs were given background colors of white, light blue, or green, and then exquisitely painted with small flower garlands. Examples of these handsome pieces with motifs of moss rosebuds, field-flower garlands, or quaint musical instruments may be seen today in various museums.

This painted Georgian furniture is rare because of the recent vogue for scraping down to the bare wood any piece that could possibly be considered antique. Many fine painted chairs have given up their decoration forever under paint-remover applied with devastating thoroughness by eager amateurs. The craze for refinishing old furniture in natural wood, with no regard for the idea of the original designer, has indeed destroyed much fine workmanship that should have been preserved.

The painted chair which lends itself best to amateur decoration is the wooden country chair, often called a kitchen chair. Simpler in design than the

great English cabinetmakers' chairs, these have painted decorations which vary with the locality. Designs from Pennsylvania, for example, combine stenciling and brush-stroke painting, and are quite different from those made in New England. Particularly noticeable is the striping technique in Pennsylvania-German decoration with bands of very wide striping in conjunction with fine narrow stripes.

Two Chair Backs:
New England (left) and Pennsylvania (right)

There is one characteristic, however, common to all the painted Early American furniture. The decoration was done with a freedom and lack of tension which we modern decorators would do well to study. Those swift steady brush strokes were, to be sure, done by a trained and skillful hand. One stroke of the striping "pencil" and the line was done. We can learn much by careful examination of the early techniques.

PRESERVING OLD DESIGNS

Many amateurs have ruined a fine example of antique painted and stenciled furniture by trying to "restore" it without any knowledge of the process by which the piece was originally decorated. The most common mistake has been an attempt to brighten up a faded bronze-stenciled design by painting over it with gold radiator paint. What pitiful results have come from this course of action! A nineteenth-century stenciled design may be restored by one method only: cutting identical stencils and applying bronze powders to the pattern in the same way that they were put on in the first place. Therefore be very slow to "touch up" any gold or silver design until you are certain of technique. Do not hesitate to consult a reputable cabinetmaker or antique dealer or your local museum to learn more about your heirloom.

If only a small part of the design is missing, it is wiser not to replace it at all. Simply clean off the pattern-area with mild soap and water, allow it to dry, and then give the whole design two coats of clear varnish, twenty-four hours apart. After the second coat is thoroughly dry, rub it with pumice and a light automobile oil to reduce the high gloss of the varnish.

An alternate method of preserving an old decoration is to give it a single coat of satin or matte varnish. This is not so bright as ordinary varnish.

When, in your opinion, the piece is in such bad condition that it should be scraped down to the bare wood, try to record the design even if only a bit of it remains. Make an accurate rendering of it on durable tracing paper and go over the penciled tracing with black ink. If there is color in the design, try to indicate the color in a second tracing. In other words, make one line drawing and one color drawing.

If you wish to learn something of the history of your chair, send the drawings you have made to me in care of the publishers of this book, and I will try to interpret the pattern in terms of the age of the piece. In any event, do file the recording of your pattern. Someday you may wish to reproduce the design either on the original piece of furniture or on another of the same period.

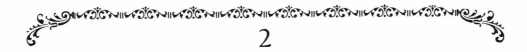

2

Terms, Materials, Surface Preparation

DECORATING TERMS

Artists-Oils or Tube-Oils: oil paint available in small tubes for decorating, art-work, and all crafts where a finely ground paint is necessary.

Bar-Top Varnishes: see *Spar and Bar-Top Varnishes.*

Bronze Stenciling: a process whereby a stencil is placed on a slightly-sticky varnished surface and the design is applied by rubbing through the holes with dry metallic powders, called bronze powders. See *Stenciling.*

Bronzing Liquids: various mediums used in the laying of gold-leaf; often called "size"; also used with metallic powders for freehand bronze painting.

Brush-Stroke Painting: decoration applied with a brush and free-flowing paint.

Built-up Stencil: see *Many-Unit or Built-up Stencil.*

Enamel-Undercoat: a "flat" paint, available mostly in white. A basic flat paint which may be tinted with tube-oils to match any color scheme; for this reason recommended as a base-coat for light-colored chairs when ready-mixed paints are not available.

Frosted Acetate or Traceolene: an extremely thin transparent material, tougher than tracing paper, used for recording antique patterns.

Gold-Leaf: a fine sheet of pure gold hammered so thin as to wrinkle at the slightest touch. It comes in small booklets with a backing of tissue on each leaf. When used for decoration it provides a depth and brilliance greater than that of bronze stenciling.

Japan Paints: more finely-ground, more transparent paints than artists-oils: especially recommended for brushwork and striping.

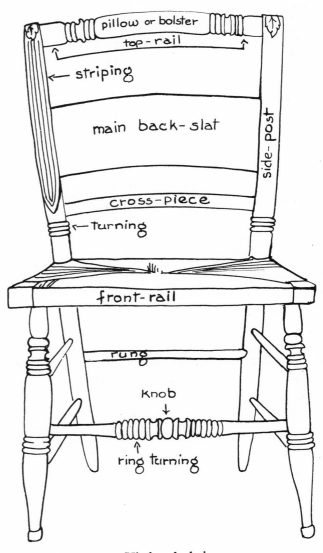

Hitchcock chair

Lithopone: a powdered white chalklike substance valuable as a tracing medium.

Many-Unit or Built-up Stencil: a stencil-design which is assembled by placing small units together and is gradually built up by partial stenciling of the units to give the effect of one object lying behind another. The built-up stencil is the highest art-form developed in bronze stenciling.

Matte Varnish: see *Satin or Matte Varnish.*

Metallic Powders: "gold" lining powders which are available dry and in a wide range of colors for use in bronze stenciling. "Lining" powders are finely ground and preferred for stenciling.

Reverse Stenciling: a stencil design made by placing a solid pattern on a surface and applying a bronze-powder background around it rather than applying the pattern itself in bronze.

Sandpapers: ordinary light tan sandpaper should be used only in paint-removing and preparing chairs for decorating. For all finishing work, I recommend silicon carbide, wet or dry sandpaper in 4/0 to 6/0 weight. It is reddish tan and far more satisfactory than the old-fashioned type.

Satin or Matte Varnish: a varnish containing wax to give a "rubbed-effect" finish. It is not so resistant to weather or alcohol and acids as the spars and bar-tops, but is recommended as a final finish for chairs.

Shellac: a brittle fast-drying medium excellent for sealing the pores of raw wood; not so durable as bar- or spar-top varnish. The term "1 lb. cut" means that one pound of dry flake is dissolved in one gallon of alcohol; "5 lb. cut" means five pounds of dry flake to a gallon.

Single-Unit Stencil: a stencil-design cut in a single piece and applied in one operation.

Size: the medium, usually varnish or turpentine or a combination of both, used in the laying of gold-leaf and freehand bronze painting.

Spar and Bar-Top Varnishes: slow-drying varnishes, as compared to quick-drying lacquers. These terms are almost interchangeable in decorating work, spar having high resistance to water and other moisture, and bar-top having high resistance to alcohol. Bar-top is recommended for light-colored chairs where it is important not to cause a change of color. It comes nearest to being a really clear varnish.

Steel Wool: in sizes 0 to 6/0. The coarser grades (low numbers) may be used in paint-removing, but for all finishing we recommend the superfine from 4/0 to 6/0.

Stenciling: decoration applied by means of a pattern, the units of which have been pierced by cutting. The design is placed by painting through the holes.

Stenciling in Oils: a process by which the design is applied to a surface by means of a stubby bristle brush and opaque paint.

Tack Cloth: a material commercially-treated with varnish and turpentine to be used in removing every speck of dust from a surface which is to be decorated. Not recommended in gold-leaf work.

Tacky: a term used for the exact moment of adhesiveness of varnish or size when bronze powders or gold-leaf should be applied.

Traceolene: see *Frosted Acetate.*

Tube-Oils: see *Artists-Oils.*

FURNITURE TERMS

American Empire Chair: a name given to American chairs made from 1815-1850, which show influence of the previous styles, French Empire and American Sheraton. In this category is the Hitchcock chair, which, although a sturdy and attractive chair, is not so well designed nor so old as Sheraton fancy chairs. Because they were made by the so-called "fancy-chair makers," Hitchcocks are often called fancy chairs. In my opinion, this is a slipshod and erroneous use of the term.

Arrow-back: a wooden country style chair of the Windsor family with three or four spindles shaped like arrows forming the back, *circa* 1820.

Circa or ca: from the Latin meaning "around," applied with a date to a piece of furniture to indicate, not the exact time of manufacture, but the year or years when that style of furniture was made and used, as *circa* or *ca* 1776.

Fancy Chair: an American Directory chair of the Sheraton type, originally painted and stenciled in dark, light, or "fancy" colors, made 1800-1815. Relatively few remain with original decoration.

Fiddle-back: in this book, a nineteenth-century American chair having a wide perpendicular back-slat shaped like a vase or fiddle, *circa* 1840. The term fiddle-back is also applied to antique chairs of the Queen Anne variety which have a back-slat of similar construction.

Hitchcock: see *American Empire Chair.*

Sheraton-Windsor: a name sometimes given to wooden country chairs having back spindles similar to the Windsor type, but with a wide toprail reminiscent of Sheraton fancy chair, *circa* 1820.

Thumb-back: a colloquial name for a wooden Windsor-type chair with side-posts terminating in a thumb-shaped piece.

MATERIALS

Most materials needed for refinishing and decorating chairs may be bought at an art-supply or a hardware store. If you have difficulty in securing supplies in your community, ask a local printer for the name of an art-supply house in the nearest large city. Many houses put out catalogues which they will send on request. From the catalogue every possible item for a decorator's kit may be ordered.

FOR BACKGROUND AND BASE COATS

If it is an old chair

½ pint bar-top or spar-varnish

½ pint turpentine

½ pint flat paint or enamel-undercoat (for grained wood finish in imitation-mahogany or rosewood, both red and black paint)

If it is an old chair

Paint scraper

Paint remover

Pint of denatured alcohol

Steel wool

2/0 sandpaper

6/0 superfine wet or dry sandpaper

½ lb. pumice powder or rottenstone

Rags

½ pint turpentine

½ pint spar-varnish

½ pint flat paint (for grained-wood finish in

imitation-mahogany or rosewood, both red and black flat paint or enamel-undercoat)

½ pint satin or dull-finish varnish

Brushes

2-inch bristle brush for applying background paints

1½-inch ox-hair brush for varnishing

Several French quill brushes: No. 6 to No. 9: in medium lengths

No. 3 pointed water-color brush in red or black sable

No. 12 artist's sable brush

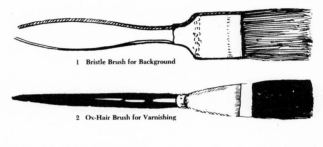

1   Bristle Brush for Background

2   Ox-Hair Brush for Varnishing

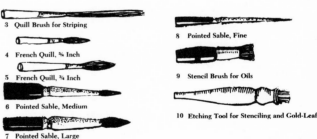

3   Quill Brush for Striping

4   French Quill, ⅜ Inch

5   French Quill, ¾ Inch

6   Pointed Sable, Medium

7   Pointed Sable, Large

8   Pointed Sable, Fine

9   Stencil Brush for Oils

10   Etching Tool for Stenciling and Gold-Leaf

FOR DECORATING

Artist-oils in tubes

White (Titanium, Philips White, or Permalba), black, Van Dyke brown, raw umber, burnt umber, burnt sienna, English vermilion, alizarin crimson, cadmium red, chrome-yellow medium, yellow ochre, chrome green, permanent green, Prussian blue, verdigris

FOR STENCILING

Architects-linen

Bronze powders (lining powders, if available, as they are of finer quality): Pale Gold, Brushed Brass, Rich Gold-Leaf, Aluminum, Silver, Fire Bronze

Sharp-pointed embroidery scissors

XACTO knife

Razor blade (double-edged, with one edge protected by adhesive tape to make a flexible tool in stencil-cutting)

Tracing paper (for transferring designs)

Frosted acetate (Super-see or Traceolene for recording designs)

Black drawing ink

Small piece of chamois or pure silk velvet

Drawing pens

Pencils

White crayon or chalk

Lithopone-powder

Stick of drawing charcoal (for working on a light-colored object)

Graphite paper (for transferring designs to light-painted furniture)

"Tack" cloth (a fabric commercially treated with varnish and turpentine for wiping a surface before stenciling)

Roll of cellophane tape

Roll of masking tape

FOR GOLD-LEAF WORK

Hiburnish Bronzing Liquid

Japan gold size

Service seal varnish

Books of leaf: Deep Gold, Palladium, Lemon

Note: In buying gold-leaf, try to procure Transfer Gold for "gilding in the wind," or Golden Touch.

CARE OF MATERIALS

BRUSHES

Your brushes will give you long and satisfactory service if you give them proper care.

While working, have at hand a pint-jar of turpentine to which you have added a teaspoon of linseed oil. Place a wad of excelsior in the bottom of the jar. After using a brush, wipe out and squeeze out excess paint onto a clean newspaper; then drop brush into the turpentine. Several brushes may be kept in the same jar. The purpose of the excelsior is to prevent the brush from standing on the floor of the jar and picking up any residue of paint.

Brushes stay in good condition in this type of container for several days. When there will be a considerable interval before you use brushes again, wash them thoroughly. Wipe off excess paint onto a clean newspaper. Rinse brush thoroughly in turpentine. Then wash out carefully in warm water and yellow soap; finally rinsing in clear warm water. Shake out excess water and allow to dry overnight while standing on handle-end in an empty jar. When dry and fluffy, wrap brush in wax paper and store in a box.

Warning: Moths dote on fine sable or camels-hair brushes. If you are storing a brush for more than a week or two, put paradichloride crystals or other moth-preventive in box.

PAINTS

Paint should not be left uncovered for any length of time. Replace cover on each can and tighten by stepping on it. Then invert the can and store it in this position to prevent "skin" from forming on surface of paint.

Artists-oils should be squeezed up from the bottom of the tube and tube rolled up as paint is used. Do not allow excess paint to accumulate at neck of tube, and screw cap firmly after use. If cap sticks and is difficult to remove, dip top of tube in very hot water to loosen.

STENCILS

Always clean stencils before putting them away. They may be quickly wiped off with carbon tetrachloride or, somewhat less effectively, with turpentine. Allow to dry, then store flat in large Manila envelopes. Label the envelope with the name of each stencil or, in the case of small units, list by number. Avoid exposing stencils to water or dampness as they are worthless if the starch is lost from the linen.

PREPARING CHAIRS FOR DECORATING

NEW CHAIRS

The porous surface of a *new* chair in natural wood requires a sealing-off coat of varnish or shellac to insure a smooth surface for the final finishing coats. This primer should be a thin even coat of clear primer made by adding 2 tablespoons turpentine and 1 tablespoon linseed oil to a half-pint of clear varnish. Shellac, thinned 25 per cent with denatured alcohol, may be substituted, but a good bar-varnish is more durable, and this is recommended.

Place the chair on a work table which has been covered with newspaper or a drop-cloth to protect it. Turn the chair upside down and begin with the bottom rungs. Dip the brush in the varnish until you have covered about one-third of the bristles. Apply the varnish evenly to legs and rungs; be certain to catch all drips with the brush so there will be no ridges or sags in the undercoats.

Now place the chair upright and varnish the top, back, and sides. Do the seat last. Then, as you work, you will always have a dry place to grasp.

Allow the priming coat to dry thoroughly. The next day give the chair a coat of flat oil paint or "enamel-undercoat" in the color of your choice. Avoid high-gloss paints and quick-drying enamels as a too-shiny finish does not lend itself well to decoration. After 24 hours, if the first coat of paint seems completely dry, give the chair a second coat of the same color.

Any chair you paint should have at least two coats of basic color. Avoid having the paint too thick or you will obscure delicate knobs and turnings. They must have thin even coats. Thin the paint with turpentine if it seems too heavy. Never use a water-base paint for furniture; oil paints are more durable.

After the second coat of paint is dry, apply a coat of clear varnish before you begin to decorate. The reason for this is that any mistakes in drawing or painting are more easily rectified on a slick surface than on the dull matte surface of flat paint.

The flat surface absorbs your mistakes; the slick surface tosses them off.

OLD CHAIRS

It is not easy to make an all-inclusive statement as to how to tackle the refinishing of an *old* chair. So much depends on the state of repair of the piece in question. The first rule is to be certain the chair is firm and structurally able to bear weight and otherwise perform its function of being a resting place for the body. However, all chairs that wobble are not suffering from joint trouble. Sometimes a tight new cane or rush seat will restore firmness and stability.

A chat with one of the workmen in the present Hitchcock chair factory at Riverton, Connecticut throws light on methods used in early chairmaking and explains why a hundred-year-old wooden chair often shows no sign of weakened joints. In making the lower half of the chair, green lumber was used for the legs while the rungs were made of well-seasoned wood. As the green wood lost its moisture with the passage of time, the leg of the chair shrank a little causing the socket around the rung to get tighter and tighter. It was not necessary to use glue with this form of rung-and-socket construction, so there was no glue to dry out, crack, or lose its effectiveness as the years went by.

If careful examination convinces you that rungs and sockets have really come to a parting of the ways, do have a professional repair job done to restore the strength of the chair. In this case, making the chair firm calls for the use of hot animal glue, heavy wire cord, and strong vises to hold joints tightly in place until the glue dries. Anything less than a thorough job is a waste of effort if the chair is really to be used. The cost of professional work of this kind is reasonable compared to the amount of effort necessary for the amateur to accomplish good results. However, if there is a woodworking hobbyist in your home with tools and equipment and above all patience to do a painstaking repair job, turn the chair over to him before you give vent to your artistic impulses with paints or stencils. It is too bad to spend hours beautifying a chair that cannot stand firmly on its four legs.

If there is a remnant of a stenciled or painted design, however small, try to record it by tracing or copying it and coloring the pattern as accurately as you can. If the existing design is almost complete and is only partly obliterated, do not try to restore it. Give it a coat of varnish to prevent further disintegration. (See Chapter 1, section Preserving Old Designs.)

If very large areas of the chair show cracked

paint or loosened varnish and designs have deteriorated past saving, you will probably need to use both sandpaper and paint-remover to bring the surface to a point where you may safely repaint the base coat. It is not necessary in most cases to scrape the entire chair to the bare wood, but every bit of loose or cracked paint must be removed. Then sand down the remainder until the entire surface is satin smooth.

If you are not satisfied with a partial removal of the old finish by sanding, a complete job of stripping should be done with paint-remover. (See also Step-by-Step Preparation for Decorating.)

After paint has been removed and the chair is smooth and clean, you may discover cracks or nail holes that need to be covered.

STEP-BY-STEP PREPARATION FOR DECORATING

NEW CHAIRS

Priming

Apply varnish—2 tablespoons turpentine and 1 tablespoon linseed oil added to each ½ pint; or as a substitute, shellac thinned 25 percent with denatured alcohol.

1. Use a medium-sized varnish brush.

2. Work with chair at arm level. Place it on a table protected with paper. Do rungs first, seat last, for easier handling.

3. Keep priming coat thin, and rework constantly with brush to prevent sags or waves in varnish coat. Allow to dry.

Background Coat

1. Apply two coats of flat paint in color of your choice.

2. Use a medium-sized household paintbrush. Do not fill too full of paint.

3. Keep the first coat thin and rework sags as the paint runs dow and collects in waves. Allow to dry for 24 hours.

4. Apply a second thin coat of paint in exactly the same way. Allow to dry for 24 hours.

5. Give the entire chair a coat of spar- or bar-varnish.

6. Go over chair lightly with fine sandpaper or steel wool.

Note: There are decorators who insist that a priming coat is not necessary even on new porous wood. They claim success in painting the first coat directly on the wood. I have worked with and without a priming coat, and sometimes an uneven absorption of paint occurs when wood has not been primed. For best results I recommend a primer.

OLD CHAIRS

Stripping

Be sure chair is sturdy not wobbly. Have cane or rush seat in good condition. (See Preparing Chairs for Decorating.)

1. Apply a good-quality paint-remover and carefully follow directions on can.

2. Flow on with an old brush.

3. Wait until old finish wrinkles and softens. (It may take two or three applications.)

4. Scrape softened paint with metal scraper and clean surface by wiping with rags.

5. Clean out rungs and turnings with steel wool, or a jack-knife blade.

6. Wipe whole surface with clean rags and plenty of turpentine. The new electric scrapers are valuable for removing stubborn patches of paint.

Note: When chair is clean, destroy all oily rags and papers. They are fire hazards. Also be cautious in using inflammable paint-removers. Protect your hands with gloves.

Filling Holes and Cracks

1. Make a paste of iron glue and powdered pumice tinted with oil-paints to match background color.

2. Fill up the cavities, smoothing off with a small wooden spatula.

3. Wipe off excess glue with a cloth before it gets dry.

4. Smooth area around repair work with sandpaper if it remains bumpy after glue has dried.

Sanding

When all traces of paint-remover have been cleaned off and chair is dry, sand down to a smooth surface using 2/0 to 6/0 paper.

Background Coat

Proceed as for new chairs. If most of chair is still covered with a smooth well-sanded paint or varnish coat, priming coat may be omitted.

3

Background Finishes

IN EXAMINING American antique chairs, I am always impressed with the great variety of finishes which were used by early craftsmen. Not only were painted finishes in great favor, but wood painted to imitate a more expensive grain was common. Here we shall discuss several types of background-painting and include directions for natural-wood finishes as well.

A common practice of early craftsmen was to deepen the grain on plain woods to simulate costly crotch-mahogany or curly maple. Artificial graining also made it possible to work in various woods that did not match. Imitation-rosewood finish was a favorite.

IMITATION-ROSEWOOD FINISH

This background is particularly recommended for Hitchcock chairs and Boston rockers, but if you do not care for imitation graining, it is in keeping with the period to have an all-black finish. Remember, however, that the grained finish is much improved by a coat of varnish. Right after application, the flat-black looks lusterless. Later, finishing coats of varnish bring life and light to the black.

The main back-slat, which carries the stenciled design, is usually painted solid black on old chairs. The reason for this is that black makes the most effective background for gold stenciling, although there are chairs to be found in which the main-slat, carrying the stencils, is grained like the rest of the chair. Decide on the way you like it and paint according to your preference.

Try to examine an antique chair with imitation graining before you decorate your own piece. Although graining is not difficult to do, the beginner may be helped by studying firsthand the technique of old chairmakers in applying black over red.

STEP-BY-STEP FOR IMITATION-ROSEWOOD FINISH

1. Give priming coat of varnish or shellac thinned out with turpentine.

   a. Use a varnish brush with bristles about 1½ inches long and 1 inch wide.

   b. Let dry overnight.

2. Apply a coat of Venetian red or Chinese red. Since this is an undercoat, the exact shade is not important so long as it is bright red. Avoid high-gloss enamel. A flat or semigloss paint is better.

   a. Use a bristle paint brush about 2½ inches long and 1½ inches wide.

   b. Be sure paint is well stirred and no thicker than thin cream.

   c. After 20 minutes, retouch with an almost-dry brush to remove waves or sags which may have formed in paint-coat.

   d. Let dry overnight.

3. (Optional) If red coat seems thin or uneven, give the chair a second coat of the same color. If you have a firm even red surface, omit the second coat.

4. Apply a coat of flat-black over the red and, before the black is dry, quickly wipe out wavy sweeps or patches of the black paint to give a mottled effect. You are trying to get the look of wood-graining by uncovering just enough red base to make it glow beneath the black. For wiping use a piece of coarse-grained mosquito netting or an almost-dry paintbrush. I have sometimes used an old comb to get a fine-grained effect. Let your imagination guide you; you may show as much or as little red as you wish. Let dry thoroughly.

5. Give two thin coats of bar-top varnish, 24 hours apart. Rub lightly with steel wool between coats.

6. Rub final coat down with steel wool or 6/0 sandpaper.

7. Polish with crude oil.

Alternate treatment

Give a coat of dull-finish or satin-varnish, and do not rub down with sandpaper.

STEP-BY-STEP FOR MAHOGANY OR WALNUT GRAIN

1. Apply priming coat, as in Wax Finish, page 28. Allow to dry.

2. Use flat-black paint, to which a small amount of Indian red has been added. With a pointed sable brush, paint in imitation grain by means of lines, streaks, and whorls. Allow to dry.

3. Apply a coat of varnish deepened by the addition of burnt sienna and burnt umber until it is a medium brown. For best effect the varnish coat should not be in too sharp contrast to the black graining. If graining seems too noticeable, add more burnt umber to the varnish coat and let dry thoroughly.

4. Rub down with sandpaper and steel wool.

5. Apply a coat of satin-varnish.

6. Paint main back-slat solid black, if chair is to be stenciled. This was usually done in the brown-over-black grained finish. This plain surface makes a better background for receiving the gold stencil.

STEP-BY-STEP FOR CURLY OR BIRDS-EYE MAPLE

1. Apply sealing coat as in Wax Finish page 28. Allow to dry.

2. Mix burnt sienna, yellow ochre, and burnt umber in ½ cup mixed varnish and turpentine, keeping burnt sienna the dominant tone.

3. For *curly maple*, dip a flannel rag into the mixture and rub over the chair, allowing the color to remain more heavily in some places than others to indicate the ripple and curl.

4. For *birds-eye maple*, rub color over entire chair, allowing certain areas to remain lighter than others. Indicate point or birds-eye by means of the eraser-end of a pencil dipped in the paint and applied to the still-wet color background with a twirling motion. If possible, obtain a sample of genuine curly or birds-eye maple to copy grain.

5. *Alternate treatment:* Paint entire surface white or ivory. When dry, follow directions as in 2, 3 and 4.

6. When chair is dry, apply two coats shellac or varnish 24 hours apart. If the priming coat was shellac, use shellac for finishing. If priming coat was varnish, use varnish for final finish.

OTHER PAINTED FINISHES

There is no treatment for an odd assortment of chairs, tables, or chests of drawers that serves to pull them together decoratively so well as the satin-black finish. Set off with a simple design or gold border, furniture of almost any period or design may thus be integrated into a pleasing unit. The classic motifs of laurel wreath, leaf border, Greek key, or fruit garlands lend themselves well to the black background. Every sort of bronze-stencil design is also appropriate on a black background.

STEP-BY-STEP FOR SATIN-BLACK FINISH

1. Apply priming coat as in Wax Finish, page 28. Allow to dry.

2. Give two coats flat-black, allowing at least 24 hours drying-time between coats. Flat-black, because of high wax content, dries in a very short time, but if a second coat is applied before the first has completely dried, it may show welts that are difficult to remove.

3. Give coat of bar-top or spar-varnish. Allow to dry well.

4. Rub down with 4/0 sandpaper. Dust off.

5. Apply motif of your choice in gold or other colors, see page 43.

6. For a final finish apply a coat of satin-varnish. (This comes in various degrees of matte or dull finish. Ask for one that is very dull. Satin-varnish should always remain the final coat; do not put one coat of it on top of another.) If the surface seems too shiny, rub gently with 4/0 steel wool applied with automobile or lemon oil. Polish clean with soft cloth.

STEP-BY-STEP FOR LIGHT-PAINTED FINISH

1. Apply priming coat as in Wax Finish, page 28. Allow to dry.

2. Give two coats of chosen color, allowing 24 hours drying-time between coats. (Any semigloss paint which is the proper color is suitable. It is not

necessary to put a final coat of varnish over semi-gloss paint. If you wish to match a color and do not find it on the charts, use enamel-undercoat in white and tint with artists-oils to desired color.)

3. Apply a final coat of satin-varnish after decoration is completed. (In working with light backgrounds, remember that varnish makes any color slightly yellow. This is most noticeable on pure white, light blue, or other delicate pastel shades. With these add 1/3 white enamel to the enamel-undercoat. This will make it unnecessary to use varnish as a finish.)

STEP-BY-STEP FOR DARK-PAINTED FINISH

Sometimes it is difficult to find the exact shade in ready-mixed semigloss paint. If the color is available, use it directly as it comes from the can. No final varnish coats will be required. If the color is almost what you want but seems too bright, lighten it, darken it, or gray it down with artists-oils.

For darkening most colors, lamp-black mixed with a small amount of mauve is good, except with the yellows. Black makes them look muddy or green. For yellows use burnt sienna mixed with a little burnt umber.

To lighten colors, add white. If you want to soften or gray them down, add mauve to yellows, orange to blues, red to greens, and green to reds. This neutralizing or graying-down must be worked out ever so gently or the original color may rapidly lose its clear tone.

1. Apply priming coat as directed in Wax Finish, page 28.

2. Give two coats of chosen color, allowing 24 hours drying-time between coats.

3. Apply a final coat of satin-varnish, if it seems necessary for a good finish.

STEP-BY-STEP FOR THUMB-PAINTED FINISH

Swirls and whorls, fan and rope patterns were used as background-finishes for chests, tables, long benches, and chairs. The most common use of thumb-painting seems to have been on plank seats of wooden chairs and Boston rockers, although many Pennsylvania chests have fascinating and elaborate backgrounds done with thumbs or putty rolls or both. Best effects are obtained when swirl

decoration is kept in close color tone to the original background color, which was usually of brown tones on cream or light yellow.

Complete Chairs

1. Apply priming coat as in Wax Finish, page 28. Allow to dry.

2. Paint chair or settee in chosen background color, and allow to dry.

3. Mix a brown glaze by adding small quantities of burnt umber and burnt sienna to quick-drying varnish. The varnish should be only slightly colored and retain a semi-transparency.

4. Apply glaze to chair.

5. Immediately, while glaze is wet, work out patterns in swirls, whorls, or the "doodle" of your choice, using your bare thumb or a roll of putty to make the designs. Mistakes may be brushed out with a stroke of the color glaze. For this type of freehand painting, make several practice attempts before actually working on a chair.

Step-by-Step for Chair Seats

1. Paint center of chair seat in contrast to remainder of chair as in diagram. Allow to dry.

2. Apply a glaze to center part of seat only. Use a quick-drying varnish to which has been added enough burnt umber and burnt sienna to color the varnish but still leave it semi-transparent.

3. With your thumb or a roll of putty, mark off a repeat-pattern such as a fan or rope design in even rows.

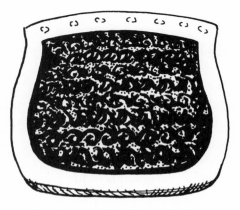

Thumb-painted finish on chair seat

Modern black paint may be "doctored" by the amateur decorator to imitate the rusty appearance of an antique-black background.

1. Recipe:
   tube burnt umber
   tube raw umber
   ½ tube burnt sienna
   ¼ tube alizarin crimson
   ¼ tube Prussian blue
   4 tablespoons turpentine
   ½ pint flat-black
   2 tablespoons white enamel-undercoat

Stir and blend first six ingredients until well mixed. Then add flat-black and enamel-undercoat. If mixture seems too thick, add a little more turpentine.

2. Apply two thin coats of antique-black, 24 hours apart, as a background for old chairs which are to be decorated with authentic antique patterns.

NATURAL-WOOD FINISHES

WAX FINISH

(Read Chapter 2, Step-by-Step Preparation for Decorating.)

Examine chair which has been sanded until smooth and decide whether wood needs to be darkened or tinted to deepened color. Mahogany, cherry, or walnut rarely need further color. Pine, birch or poplar often need an application of umber.

Coloring Coats
Old Pine Finish for Pine, Birch, or Poplar

1. Mix 2 tablespoons turpentine, 2 tablespoons varnish, and 1 teaspoon linseed oil in cup or bowl.

2. Squeeze into a saucer an inch or two of burnt umber and a smaller amount of yellow ochre. A bit of burnt sienna may be added if a reddish shade is preferred. Blend colors with a flat stick.

3. Saturate a soft flannel cloth with varnish-and-turpentine mixture and, when well moistened, dip it into the blended paint, taking up only a small amount of the paint.

4. Rub paint into surface of chair allowing enough color to remain on wood to give it a rich hue. Depth of color may be regulated by wiping

off paint with a clean rag dipped in turpentine. Final shellac and varnish coats tend to darken a chair, so allow for this in applying the burnt umber. Let dry for at least 24 hours.

Mahogany or Walnut Finish

To simulate the color of the darker woods on any of the light woods, apply a penetrating oil stain in walnut or mahogany, using a soft flannel cloth. Rub into wood and as it penetrates, rub off again until the desired color has been achieved. Allow to dry.

Priming Coat

1. Shellac

Give chair two thin coats first-quality orange shellac, diluted one quarter with denatured alcohol. Allow 24 hours drying-time between coats. Do not use shellac that has been lying around. Chemical changes sometimes cause deterioration in old shellac. It is best to discard shellac after it is six to eight months old.

2. Clear primer

A clear primer may be employed in place of shellac. Add 2 tablespoons turpentine and 1 tablespoon linseed oil to ½ pint bar-top varnish. Stir gently. (A heavy stirring will fill the varnish with small bubbles which mar the finish.) Apply the clear primer to chair. When thoroughly dry give it a second coat. Allow to dry 24 hours.

Sanding

1. Rub down with a gentle but persistent stroke using 4/0 sandpaper. When surface is quite smooth, complete the rubbing down with 4/0 steel wool. Wear an old glove when working with steel wool to protect hands.

2. Remove all traces of sanding dust and wipe clean with tack cloth or cloth moistened with turpentine.

Finishing

1. Rub entire chair with brown wax, taking care to apply only a thin coat. Allow to dry. (To make brown wax, mix ordinary paste floor wax with a small amount of burnt umber, just enough to give a brown tint. Work umber thoroughly into wax with small wooden spatula. Do not use liquid wax.)

2. When wax coat has dried for half an hour or more, rub and polish every part of chair with a soft

flannel cloth.

3. Continue these wax coats until sheen on wood is satisfactory.

LINSEED OIL FINISH

In many ways this is the simplest finish for wood because, briefly, the oil is merely rubbed into the raw wood and then rubbed off again. Nevertheless, to bring up a fine lasting polish by this method takes time and patience. The oil should be rubbed in every day or two for the first five or six applications, then applied about once a week. As the glowing polish is built up, applications of oil may be tapered off. Many people say that it takes a year of "oil and elbow" to rub into the wood a satisfactory linseed-oil finish. All seem to agree, however, that when it has finally been achieved, you have something!

There are several types of linseed oil:

1. *Raw linseed oil* is the pure oil from flax seed, extracted either by heat or pressure or both. It is sometimes refined for use in artists oil-paints by being exposed in shallow glass trays to the sun's heat. Since raw linseed oil is much more standard than the present-day boiled linseed oil, we recommend it for the beginner. Its disadvantage is a tendency to darken wood. Its light body also prevents it from giving the high polish of the more concentrated boiled oil.

2. *Boiled linseed oil* is commercially prepared in different ways, quality being dependent on the method of "boiling." There have been many commercial short cuts in producing this. Synthetics and dryers have replaced the old-time process of actually boiling the oil in great vats and allowing it to cool while still tightly covered. Some of the substances which give the tough wearing qualities are sacrificed, making the ordinary boiled linseed oil less valuable as a furniture finish. Its advantage over the raw is that it is not so prone to darken wood, and it will build up to a higher final finish.

Kettle-boiled linseed oil is not easy to obtain today. If it can be secured, it is the most valuable for a glowing lasting finish. Some furniture men say that the litho-varnish used in printing is a good substitute for kettle-boiled linseed oil. No. 3 litho-varnish probably resembles most closely genuine kettle-boiled linseed oil.

STEP-BY-STEP FOR OIL FINISH

1. Place half a pint of raw linseed oil in one jar and half a pint of turpentine in another jar and set both in a pan of hot water, and heat them a little. While it is not absolutely necessary to do this, these ingredients seem to penetrate the wood more easily if they are warm.

2. Pour turpentine into oil and mix well. A small amount of burnt umber may be added at this point but only if you want to darken the wood. Allow for the fact that with each application of oil the wood will get darker, so go lightly with the umber.

3. Using either a soft flannel cloth or your bare hand, apply a small quantity of the "oil-turps" mixture directly onto the clean raw wood and rub it in, always rubbing *against* the grain. Work fast to cover the whole surface, rubbing hard all the time. Rub until all oil has been absorbed by the wood.

Caution: Do not work on a cold or damp day if you can avoid it. Try to work out-of-doors on a bright day. If this is not feasible, choose a warm room, but be careful that it is well ventilated.

4. Repeat this process every day or so with uncolored linseed oil and turpentine until oil stays on surface of wood and is no longer absorbed. When this happens, rub off all excess oil with a dry cloth.

5. Apply oil about once a month until finish is satisfactory.

6. Be sure to destroy all oily rags. These are highly inflammable.

BLEACHED AND LIMED FINISHES

With the increased interest in contemporary and modern furniture many people are trying out the blonde or bleached finishes on woodwork and furniture. Interesting effects have been obtained, in particular with oak. Oak, one of the durable hard woods, was held in great disdain for many years because of the era of bad taste in furniture known as "Golden Oak." The new pickled, bleached, and blonde finishes have brought oak back into a vogue such as it has not had for years. These finishes are not suitable for antique chairs, but are attractive on modern styles.

STEP-BY-STEP FOR BLEACHED FINISH

1. Sand chair to a smooth surface.

2. Mix ¼ pound Savogran with 1 quart water and apply to chair with an old paint brush. Allow to dry in sun if possible. Give chair several applications until a satisfactory degree of lightness is achieved.

Savogran is the safest bleach for an amateur to use. Oxalic acid crystals are poisonous and rough on the hands, but they are an excellent bleaching agent. If you do use them, the correct proportion is ½ pound oxalic acid to 2 quarts hot water (distilled). Stir until crystals are dissolved. Allow to cool. Next dissolve ¼ pound hyposulphite of soda in 1 quart of water. Soak area to be bleached in oxalic acid; then apply soda solution. Allow to dry out of doors if possible. Repeat process if wood is not sufficiently whitened. Wash off with borax soap and water.

3. Apply a full coat of pure white shellac or bar-top varnish after either bleach.

4. Sand lightly with 4/0 sandpaper.

5. Apply a second coat of varnish.

6. When dry, rub down with steel wool and finish with a thin coat of paste wax. (Floor-wax is excellent for this.)

7. Polish with a soft cloth.

STEP-BY-STEP FOR LIMED FINISH

A satisfactory imitation of limed wood may be achieved by rubbing white enamel-undercoat into smooth raw wood and then rubbing it off. This finish is particularly recommended for oak chairs from which the golden-oak finish has been removed, or for building a contemporary patina on natural unfinished wooden furniture. It is not at all suitable for mahogany, walnut, or antique maple, although an interesting effect may be had with this treatment of knotty pine.

1. Sand surface to fine smoothness and remove sanding dust with tack cloth.

2. Dip sponge or soft cloth into white enamel-undercoat and rub into pores of raw wood, removing excess paint with a clean cloth moistened with turpentine. Leave enough paint to sink into the open grain of the wood but keep the whole effect transparent. Allow to dry.

3. Apply two coats clear bar-top varnish or white shellac, allowing 24 hours drying time between each coat.

4. When dry, rub down with 4/0 sandpaper.

5. Apply thin coat of paste wax, and, when wax is dry (in about half an hour), polish with a soft cloth. Interesting color effects may be obtained by rubbing in light blue or gray paint instead of white. Experiment in this transparent coloring of raw wood on a smooth board or wooden box before working on the final project.

ANTIQUING

STEP-BY-STEP FOR NATURAL WOOD

1. Mix a glaze of 1 part turpentine, 1 part linseed oil, and 1 part burnt umber combined with a little raw umber.

2. Rub glaze into wood and rub off before it dries, starting in center and using a circular motion. Continue applications until desired color is reached. Remember each succeeding varnish coat will darken the finish. Be careful, therefore, not to rub in too heavy a color.

STEP-BY-STEP ON PAINTED BACKGROUNDS

Prepare a glaze

1. For *dark colors*, mix a glaze of 1 part turpentine, 1 part varnish, and 1 part burnt umber combined with a small amount of burnt sienna and a speck of raw umber.

2. For *light colors* in blue or green, mix a glaze of 1 part turpentine, 1 part varnish, and a little of the original background paint, slightly darkened with lamp-black.

3. Rub glaze over entire surface, removing most of it at once, leaving only enough to dim the sharp new look of the colors. It is unwise to use antique glazes with a heavy hand. Not only does each varnish coat used in finishing darken the decoration to a degree, but time quickly dims bright colors. Enjoy the gay brightness of your decorating while you may.

4. For gold stenciling, use the glaze for dark colors.

Alternate method

1. Tint varnish with burnt umber or lamp-black and give entire chair two coats.

2. Rub down with fine steel wool or superfine sandpaper.

3. Apply a final coat of clear satin-varnish. The final coat of varnish should never contain a tint for antiquing.

Note: Burnt umber is preferred for tinting varnish when used over all red, yellow, brown, or gold tones, including bronze stenciling. Lamp-black or a small amount of the chair's background color in a darker shade is used to tint the varnish for antiquing blue, green, or aqua tones.

FINAL FINISHING

STENCILED AND PAINTED CHAIRS

1. After the pattern is stenciled on chair and striping has been completed, wash stenciled areas with water to remove loose particles of bronze powder.

2. When the chair is thoroughly dry, give a coat of spar- or bar-top varnish. Allow to dry.

3. Smooth down with 4/0 steel wool or 6/0 sandpaper.

4. Apply coat of satin-varnish.

This should complete the decorating. If the satin-varnish finish seems too shiny, rub lightly with rottenstone lubricated with a small amount of automobile oil. Polish with a soft flannel cloth.

NATURAL-WOOD CHAIRS

1. Give chair a thin coat of brown wax.

2. When dry, polish entire chair with a soft cloth. Commercial brown-wax preparations such as Minwax and Cohasset Colonial's wood finish are very satisfactory for natural-wood chairs.

4

Brush-Stroke Painting

FREEHAND or brush-stroke painting was the method used to decorate country-tin and simple furniture during most of the nineteenth century. It is a different and more artless technique than the elaborate freehand painting characteristic of the large floral trays imported from England, or made in this country between 1790 and 1840. Brush-stroke painting, as I think of it, is folk decoration in primary colors that adorns not only antique tinware but also country arrow-back, thumb-back, and other chairs made of wood.

The best brush-stroke painting is put on with great freedom and little subsequent "filling-in" of a design with the brush. For years the implement we know as an artist's paint brush was called a pencil. Old coach-stripers always spoke of their tool as a striping pencil, perhaps because they drew the design with a brush directly on the object to be decorated, with little or no guiding pattern.

For amateur brush-stroke painters I recommend some kind of line-guide, but I feel that even beginners should learn primarily to paint a design with the brush, rather than laboriously to fill in a line-drawing. Preliminary practice in perfecting a free brush-stroke is important. Here are several sample borders. Try them with your brush not once but a number of times.

PRACTICING A FREE STROKE

Dip brush in paint until it is well filled. Place it on surface lightly and, as you make the stroke, exert pressure for an instant to form the wide part of the motif, releasing the pressure at once to complete the stroke in a hairline finish. Make the stroke quickly and, above all, with a freedom of movement. After a time there will be control as well as freedom and, when this point is reached, you are ready to practice making flowers and leaves with the same brush-stroke technique. Your aim is actually to draw the form and outline with the brush rather than to fill in a drawing with paint. The tracing of the pattern makes merely a guideline for placement. You should try always in brush-stroke painting *to create the design with the paintbrush.*

SCROLLS

An even wider sweep of the brush is demanded in painting scrolls. Ideally one free stroke accomplishes each curve. Practice scrolls and curlicues with abandon in your wrist until you overcome the natural tendency of all beginners to inch timidly along the tracing line. It is helpful to examine brushwork on genuine antiques. There was a great deal of scrollwork used on Victorian painted furniture. Try to find an example of this, for one glance reveals the steady flow of line characteristic of such painting.

ELABORATELY-SHADED FLORAL DESIGNS

On some Victorian chairs, especially those in painted bedroom sets, the painting of the floral units is reminiscent of the flower designs on elaborate Chippendale trays. It is quite different from the folk-technique on tinware where flower and fruit forms were so simplified as to be stylized. This naturalistic rendering of flower sprays calls for a more studied approach. Flowers and leaves are carefully drawn and shaded so as to seem lifelike. Secondary color tones floated in varnish, layer on layer, will contribute to the natural effect, and look quite different from the naive representation of shading by one or two concise brush strokes. The floral design on the late Boston rocker (page 97), and the moss-rose pattern (page 109) are both

Practice brush strokes

painted in the naturalistic style; specific instructions are included with each.

STRIPING

The technique of striping is the same as for brush-stroke painting because the so-called "striper's pencil" was in reality a quill-brush, often with hair 2 inches long.

Authentic color formulas

Yellow was by far the most common color used for striping. Although some dark chairs were striped in off-white, yellow seems to have been the favorite for all types of furniture. Here is a recipe for an authentic striping-yellow:

    1 part chrome-yellow medium in Japan
    1 part yellow ochre in Japan
    small quantity of burnt sienna
    small quantity burnt umber
    1 to 2 teaspoons spar-varnish

Note: Burnt umber and burnt sienna darken a color so rapidly that it is wise to add them sparingly. The striping color should have enough of the two yellows to be bright rather than muddy in tone. The painting mixture should be well blended with a spatula to the consistency of light cream.

Green: add small amount of lamp-black to chrome green.

Brown: combine burnt sienna, yellow ochre, and black.

Blue: use Prussian blue with touch of white and black.

White: add touch of burnt sienna and mauve.

The important thing to remember is that striping should be in sharp contrast to background color. Remember that the finishing coats of varnish will somewhat reduce the intensity of the stripe, so do not dull it too much.

Applying the Stripe

1. Be sure surface to be striped has had a coat of varnish and is thoroughly dry. It is easier to correct mistakes on a shiny surface than on flat paint.

2. Dip brush to hilt in paint.

3. Stroke brush on practice paper to expel excess paint.

4. Grasp the short stem of the long quill-brush

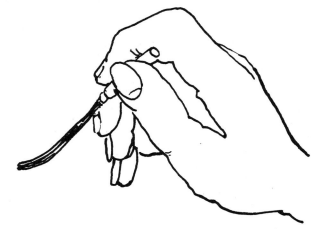

Start of Striping Stroke

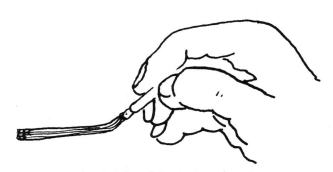

Finish of Striping Stroke

between thumb and first two fingers. Steady your hand with little finger on the edge of area to be striped. Place brush lightly on surface and draw the brush toward you, keeping your eye on the guide line just *in front of* brush, not on the brush. If you can relax and pull the striping brush toward you without becoming nervous, the chances are that, after a few tries, an acceptable stripe will be achieved. The old carriage-stripers, who developed the art of striping to such a high point, spent years perfecting their striping skill. Do not give up if your first efforts at striping appear somewhat wavering.

5. Two strips of masking-tape pasted 1/8 to 1/4 inch apart, depending on width of stripe you want, can often substitute for the hand-drawn line. A

freehand line is to be preferred, if it can be managed. Some decorators find it helpful to place a ruler parallel to line to be striped, but at least half an inch away, so that paint does not come in contact with it. The ruler serves as an eye-guide in drawing a straight striping line.

Note: If it seems easier to manipulate the striping brush by attaching it to a handle rather than by grasping it by the short quill, by all means use a handle. There are no rules which suit all craftsmen. In teaching painting techniques, I can only suggest various ways. In the actual practice of a craft, it is the workman who evolves his own easiest method of producing the desired result.

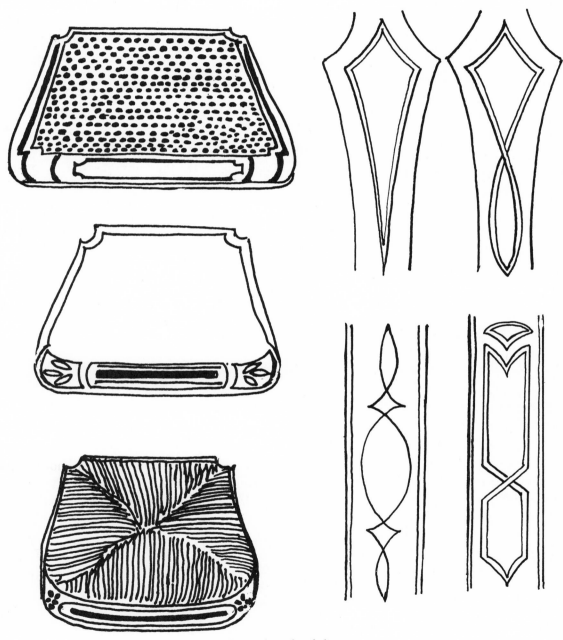

Examples of striping

[35]

5

Stenciling Techniques

STENCILING is the method of transferring a design by rubbing paint or bronze powders through cut-out sections of a master pattern. The art of stenciling is very old, and may be considered one of the earliest art-crafts known to man. Early examples have been found on walls in an ancient cave in Tibet, where large areas are covered with a repeat pattern of the Buddha motif.

In the Polynesian Islands women have used primitive stencils to make decorative borders on their skirts and scarves. The Japanese often used stenciling on cloth in conjunction with gold-thread embroidery, and examples of stenciling from elaborately-cut patterns may be seen on fabric that dates back to the eighth and ninth centuries. The wood block and the stencil were much used in France, and all over Europe the stencil appears as a means of giving pattern to wall and fabric for both secular and religious usage. Ancient hymn books and books of the Mass were made almost entirely by means of stencils, with cuttings for both lettering and musical notes.

In this country, early settlers depended on the journeyman-stenciler for beautifying their homes from floor to ceiling. Even today there are to be seen in country houses in New England well-preserved examples of stenciled wall-coverings and patterned floors. It was easier to hire an itinerant artist to transfer designs from his stencil kit than to send abroad for a wool rug or a French hand-blocked wallpaper.

Early in the nineteenth century in America gold stenciling or bronze stenciling, as it is more often called, was in vogue as ornamentation for chairs and other furniture. About 1828 the Hitchcock-type chair became popular and one of the most

fascinating and highly-developed uses of the stencil is seen in gilded decoration on these chairs. Today this chair is enjoying a great revival. The old Hitchcock factory has reopened and beautiful new Hitchcock chairs are being made and decorated from the old patterns. Natural-wood reproductions of the chairs are available and they have become popular with the amateur decorator as dining chairs or side chairs.

Natural finish Hitchcock chair ready for decorating

Complete directions for decorating a Hitchcock chair will be found on page 82. Here only the stencil itself and methods of stenciling are discussed. The gold-stenciling technique used on furniture is simply the application of bronze powder through the pierced pattern of a stencil to a tacky varnished surface on which the powder adheres and forms the design.

MATERIALS FOR STENCILING.

Architects-linen

The best material from which to make stencils for furniture is architects-linen. Stencils for antique chairs were cut from heavy rag paper, often actual sheets from ledger books, and many of these discolored old cuttings are in good condition after a hundred years. For the modern decorator, however, architects-linen or transparent tracing cloth makes a more satisfactory medium for stencil cutouts. It is tough and transparent with one dull surface and one glossy, and the design may be traced directly on its dull side from an old or new pattern.

Bronze Powders

Metallic powders in a rainbow array may be seen in art-supply stores. The important colors to buy are the various shades of gold and silver. If you intend to decorate a great variety of objects with stenciling, you may care to invest in the red, blue, green, lavender, or pink metallic powders. It is fun to experiment with several colors, and interesting effects may be attained with these more modern shades. The early gilders who did not have such a wide choice of colored powders used only shades of gold and silver with some red, and where color was necessary, applied a varnish coat tinted with transparent-oil color.

Bronze powders have various trade names, such as Pale Gold, Rich Gold, Lemon Gold, Gold-Leaf Powder, Aluminum Powder. The richest of these are Gold-Leaf and Aluminum. They are the most intense and also the most difficult to erase if they spill. Both are indispensable for stenciling. With Pale Gold, Gold-Leaf, and Aluminum powders you can reproduce almost any design in bronze stenciling, adding necessary color by an overtinting of transparent oil-paint. The "lining" golds are the most satisfactory. Although they are slightly more expensive they are more finely ground and give better results.

METHOD OF APPLYING STENCILS

In bronze stenciling the design is applied by first placing the stencil on a slightly-damp varnished surface, and firmly rubbing the metallic powder through the holes. The moment for stencil-ing occurs when the varnish has dried to just the degree of dampness known as "tacky"; that point when, in touching the surface with your finger tip, you feel a slight pull but the finger does not actually stick. Tacky varnish makes gold powder adhere and, when the stencil is lifted, the gilt imprint remains. It is always a pleasure and a surprise to the beginner to lift the first stencil and see how quickly and neatly the gold powder has transferred a design.

PALETTE FOR BRONZE POWDERS

To make a working palette for bronze powders, use a rather heavy piece of upholsterer's velour. A flat tin box makes a convenient receptacle for keeping the powders in order. Cut a piece of velour exactly the size of the bottom of the box. Pour small

Palette box for bronze powders—3-inch size

mounds of the various powders in rows on the velour, keeping the mounds about three inches apart. Cut another piece of velour the same size, to fit, nap side down, over the heaps of powder. This keeps powders from spilling or mixing with each other when you close the box, and allows you to have your bronze-powder palette easily available for stenciling.

TRANSPARENT OILS FOR OVERPAINTING

All overpainting of gold stenciling, whether to deepen the shadow sections or to add color to the design, must be done with the so-called transparent oil-paints: Alizarin crimson, Prussian blue, verdigris (greenish-blue), yellow lake, mauve, burnt sienna, raw umber, burnt umber. The last four colors are really semitransparent and do not cover heavily enough to obscure the gold. They are applied with varnish; depth of color is regulated by the amount of varnish used to thin out the color. In most cases it is best to use considerably more varnish than paint to keep a clear transparent tint for the overlay.

Care of Stencils

Stencils should be carefully cleaned after each use. Wipe them off on both sides with carbon tetrachloride or a cloth moistened with turpentine. *Never use water to clean stencils.* Water ruins tracing cloth as it causes buckling and rippling.

STEP-BY-STEP DIRECTIONS FOR STENCILING

CUTTING THE STENCIL

1. Place architects-linen, shiny side down, over pattern and trace the design.

a. Use a medium-hard pencil or a pen and black drawing ink. Make the tracing sharp and accurate to insure a neat clear stencil.

2. Cut out each segment of the design.

a. Use a razor blade or small sharp-pointed

Stencil Before and After Cutting

scissors or alternate the two. Practice will develop your cutting technique. Manicure scissors are good for rounded outlines.

b. Use commercial punch for small holes in the design, a large darning needle for the tiniest

holes. Smooth out these holes on the reverse side by rubbing with very fine sandpaper.

c. To mend broken "bridges" caused by accidental cutting, cover both sides of stencil, where break occurs, with gummed cellophane tape and recut that portion.

d. To cut stems and tendrils in a design, slit one side of stem with razor blade and cut the other side with scissors. A stencil knife is also satisfactory for use in cutting stencils, but the double-edge razor blade, with one edge protected by a binding of adhesive tape, is a handy flexible tool and is my favorite implement.

3. Test stencil, when cutting is complete, by placing it on a piece of black paper. The entire design should show through the stencil as if it were a silhouette.

VARNISHING

1. Clean thoroughly the surface to be decorated. It is impossible to be too emphatic about the need for working with clean tools on dust-free surfaces. Dust is the bane of all decorators, and future trouble with final varnish coats is avoided if meticulous care is taken to apply clean varnish with a clean brush to a clean surface.

2. Give surface to be decorated a thin coat of spar- or bar-varnish.

a. Avoid quick-drying varnishes or lacquers as a base for stenciling; they are less durable.

b. If there are any lumps, particles, or jelly-like substances in the varnish, strain it through two thicknesses of an old nylon stocking.

c. Do not dip brush into varnish can. Pour into another can just enough varnish for the project and cover the original can tightly. Exposure to air causes varnish to skim over and jell.

d. While working keep container of varnish in a bowl of warm water. Varnish flows more readily when warm.

3. Allow the varnished surface to become "tacky" or almost dry before applying stencil. This usually takes about 30 minutes on a clear sunny day. A moist rainy atmosphere will extend the drying time to such an extent that I recommend varnishing only on days when there is a minimum

of humidity.

Experience alone will be your guide to discovery of the exact state of adhesiveness known as tacky, when varnish is exactly right for gold powder. If the surface is too damp, the stencil will stick and you may find bits of linen thread remaining in the pattern. If the varnish is too dry, gold powders will not adhere. You will have to learn to know the right moment by testing the tacky varnish with your finger tip. It should feel gently adhesive. If your finger tip sticks, varnish needs more drying time.

Should varnish become too dry to hold powders, wait 24 hours, wipe excess powder from pattern with a damp cloth, and revarnish the whole surface.

To extend the drying time of varnish and prolong the period of tackiness, add a small amount of turpentine or a few drops of linseed oil to the varnish. This procedure is recommended where a large surface is to be stenciled by the built-up stencil method.

Applying the bronze powders

APPLYING BRONZE POWDERS

1. Collect the equipment; have velour palette dressed with small mounds of various shades of powder.

2. Place cut-out stencil on tacky surface, and hold firmly in position with left hand.

3. Rub bronze powder over the holes in stencil, working from outside toward center to avoid seeping of powder under edges of stencil cut-outs. Use a circular motion and polish as you rub. Cover your forefinger with a suede glove finger or wrap it in a piece of silk velvet.

4. After design is transferred, lift stencil carefully from design surface to avoid spilling any excess powder onto tacky varnish.

5. When varnish has become thoroughly dry, wipe over whole design with a damp cloth to remove excess powder before giving final varnish coats.

STEP-BY-STEP MOLDING OF LIGHT AND SHADOW

This technique is used with built-up stencils, especially of fruit and flower groups where the design is assembled by placing small units together so as to suggest light and shade and a third dimension.

Shadow and depth shown by built-up stenciling
Leaf shows veining added by means of S-curve

If you can examine examples of genuine old stenciling, you will observe the delicacy with which early workers modeled high lights and shadows. The professional effect which they obtained is the result of polishing the gold powder with a gentle rotary motion as it was applied, thus insuring a permanent contact with the varnish and a smooth burnished surface of decoration.

1. *For large fruits; as apples or pears*

a. Place stencil in position and rub a high light at the top center of the fruit.

b. Suggest the rounded form of fruit by rubbing gold powder around inside edge of the stencil cutting.

c. Emphasize upper left area on a fruit with more gold powder, allowing the lower right to drift into shadow.

2. *For bunch of grapes*

a. Place a large grape stencil in position near

the top of the place where the bunch is to be. Rub a small high light in top left corner of stencil, and suggest outline of each grape by rubbing powder around inside edge of stencil.

b. Move the stencil, and complete two or three more grapes in this same manner.

c. Suggest the remaining grapes in the bunch by stenciling only the lower half or the upper half of some grape outlines so as to give an effect of depth to the cluster.

3. *For strawberries*

a. Place unit of stem- and seed-markings in place, as in Pattern 6, and rub Aluminum Powder over it, making no attempt at shading.

b. Superimpose the outline of whole berry over the stenciled seed-markings and rub gold powder lightly over it, working from outside toward center. Allow the lower right portion of berry to remain in shadow. The heavy stenciling of seeds and leaf-cap, done in Aluminum Powder, will show through the gold-powder stenciling.

Note: For convenience, two units of strawberries are cut on one piece of stencil linen. It is also customary to cut leaves and veinings on a single piece of linen.

Leaf and vein cut on one stencil

4. *For leaves*

a. Place the veining stencil in position first and rub over the Aluminum Powder, making no effort at shading.

b. Place cut-out of the whole leaf over the stenciled vein and rub in gold powder, working from outer edge of leaf toward the center. Leave the central section of the leaf in shadow to show off veining.

c. To suggest veining by means of modeling, reverse procedure and stencil the cut-out of the whole leaf first, leaving the center in shadow. For the veining, place the S-curve, which you have cut on outer edge of stencil, on shadowy center of leaf and rub gold powder along one edge. Move the S-curve about to suggest branching veins.

5. *To suggest shadow with a single-unit design*

a. Place stencil on tacky varnished surface and secure in position with masking tape. Do not attach tape to tacky varnish if it is possible to avoid doing so. (When stenciling small units of a design, it seems easier to hold stencil firmly in place with the left hand than to use masking tape.)

b. Rub on gold powder with your velvet-covered finger, taking care to use the gold powder as a modeling medium for high lights and shadows. With grapes or other fruits and leaves, rub the gold powder solidly on the high-lighted part, and let it trail off until the shadowy area of the fruit is almost as dark as the background. Leaves are left dark in the middle and given form later by superimposing a stencil of veins.

TINTING GOLD STENCILING WITH TRANSPARENT OILS

1. Examine stenciled design to be certain it is dry. Wipe off any excess powder with a damp cloth.

2. Mix the color of your choice with a small amount of varnish, thinning it out to the proper shade with more varnish. Use an old saucer as a palette or a small bottle cap. (Be sure you are using *transparent-oil*. Opaque-oil color used for this technique would completely destroy the effect of a gold design shining through tinted overtones.) See Page 37.

3. Dip a ¾-inch quill-brush or medium-sized sable brush into paint-and-varnish mixture. With a wide sweeping motion paint over the stencil.

Note: In old stencil designs the overpainting was put on in long careless strokes with little regard for staying within the lines of the design. A small flower was apparently completed with one swift

Black undercoat for gold stenciling. Top: *Left*, complete drawing of pattern. *Right*, outline as it is to be transferred to chair. Bottom: *Left*, outline as it is filled with black. *Right*, units for assembling pattern.

circular stroke of alizarin crimson or Prussian blue. There was no painting of separate petals or leaves.

4. Deepen shadow sections by overpainting with burnt sienna mixed with a small amount of burnt umber in a little varnish. Use the same technique of a free-sweeping stroke to apply this shadow color, allowing color to fade off as it approaches lighter part of pattern.

5. Enhance veining in leaves and petals by suggesting a shadow line on one side only. Use the same dark brown, and apply with a ⅝-inch pointed quill-brush. This shading technique may also be used on gold-leaf.

BLACK UNDERCOATING

To give depth and substance to gold stenciling on a light background, give the exact area where the design is to be placed an undercoating of black **paint.**

1. Make a line-tracing of the outside edge of the *Practice Pattern: Black Undercoat for Gold Stenciling, Unit B.*

2. Transfer line-tracing to the surface to be stenciled, by means of graphite paper. Place the graphite paper in the exact spot where the design is to be. Place the line-tracing on the graphite paper and with a hard pencil draw the design. (After you remove the tracing and graphite paper, an outline of the design will remain on the surface, ready to be filled in solidly with black paint.)

3. Use a medium-sized sable brush or a ¾-inch quill and fill in the outline carefully with flat-black paint. Design should look like a silhouette. Allow

[41]

the design to dry for 24 hours.

4. Apply a thin coat of varnish to the silhouette. When varnish reaches tacky stage, you are ready to stencil.

5. Cut the units in Fig. 4 and use them to practice this technique.

a. Place the units of the *apple*, Fig. 1, and *peach*, Fig. 2, first in building up this pattern, and apply the bronze powders, as in Step-by-Step Molding of Light and Shadow.

b. Build up *grapes*, using first the large grapes, Fig. 3, and finishing the cluster with the small ones, Fig. 4. Overlap the fruit in such a way that no black spaces show, and the design is a solid mass of fruit and leaves.

c. Place the *simple leaf*, Fig. 5, stencil just above the apple.

d. Using the *more elaborate leaf*, Fig. 6, stencil the remainder of the background. By holding the leaf in various positions, and stenciling each position, the effect of massed foliage is achieved, as in Fig. 1.

When design is complete, none of the black background should be seen. It has served only to give greater depth and brilliance to the stenciling.

REVERSE STENCILING

The reverse process differs from ordinary stenciling in that the background is cut away, leaving the pattern. Usually segments of the pattern are cut out, leaving the background.

1. Cut the pattern as a silhouette instead of perforating it.

2. Place the pattern in position on tacky varnish, as in regular stenciling, and rub in a cloudy bronze-powder background. When the stencil is lifted, the pattern will appear in reverse.

FINAL VARNISH COAT

1. Examine design to be certain it is dry. If it has been executed entirely in gold powders and has no

Reverse stenciling

overpainting of transparent-oils, wash design with a damp cloth to remove excess gold powder. If design has been overpainted, it is not necessary to wipe it off. Be sure overpainting has dried thoroughly.

2. Give entire design a thin coat of spar-varnish and allow to dry for 24 hours.

3. Apply a second thin coat of varnish.

4. When second coat is thoroughly dry, rub lightly with 6/0 garnet paper.

5. Dust off and apply a final coat of satin-varnish. (For this coat any dull-finish or matte varnish is satisfactory.)

6. For tinware and other objects which require a hard waterproof surface, do not use satin-varnish for the final coat. Substitute at least two more coats of spar-varnish and a final rubbing down of pumice and oil or rottenstone and oil. Use a medium-heavy automobile oil.

OIL-STENCILING TECHNIQUE

The use of a yellow oiled-paper stencil and opaque oil-paint, applied with a stiff brush, is an acceptable method of decorating, but it is not an Early American technique. For step-by-step directions, see Pattern 13.

6

Gold-Leaf and Other Techniques

MANY nineteenth-century fancy chairs were made richer by the use of gold-leaf to heighten the effect of bronze stenciling. In particular the cornucopia-backs, which had a carved middle-slat representing a horn of plenty, were decorated with gold-leaf. On early Hitchcocks, we often find a honeysuckle or anthemion design painted in gold-leaf on the pillow or bolster toprail.

Gold was sometimes enhanced after its application by shading in tones of burnt sienna or umber, or by etching and crosshatching with fine black lines for which an etching tool or pen was used. On many black-painted chairs, classical motifs and simple borders were done entirely in gold-leaf. From earliest time, gold-leaf has had an aura of elegance. It is associated with formality and should not be used to decorate a simple country-type chair. Gold-leaf is also one of the more difficult techniques, and we suggest that a beginner learn simple bronze stenciling as preliminary training to gilding or the laying of gold-leaf.

SIZING

"Size" is the term for the varnish which makes a design-surface sticky enough to hold gold-leaf. There are many adequate sizes—varnish, glue, gum arabic, and the various prepared bronzing liquids. For the amateur's use, I recommend any good varnish prepared as a gilding size, such as Hastings Gold Size, Hiburnish Bronzing Liquid, Amber Japan, and Nonpareil. A thin coat of ordinary spar-varnish would be an adequate size for gold-leaf if the area which is to be decorated is small. My favorite size is one perfected by Esther Stevens Brazer. It consists of equal parts Hiburnish Bronzing Liquid and slow-drying varnish.

GOLD-LEAF

Gold- or silver-leaf may be bought at art-supply stores in a variety of shades, ranging from deep gold to pale lemon. The books are a little over three inches square with a thin sheet of tissue above and below each sheet of metal leaf. Recently a form of gold-leaf has come on the market which, although slightly more expensive, is much easier for a novice to handle. The metal-leaf has paper on both sides, thin tissue on one and waxed paper on the other. This type of leaf may be cut with scissors, with less danger of having it wrinkle or blow away. It may be picked up on the waxed-paper side and applied directly to the design-surface. It is called Patent Transfer Gold, for "gilding in the wind." Another easy-to-use leaf is Golden Touch. If it can be procured, it is a real short cut.

STEP-BY-STEP FOR GOLD-LEAF
TRANSFERRING THE PATTERN

1. Trace a pattern from this book or from the back of an antique chair onto transparent tracing paper.

2. Apply white chalk or lithopone-powder to back of pattern, spreading powder evenly with wad of cotton.

3. Place tracing in position on *clean* and *dry* chair-slat, or wherever the design is to be placed. With a medium-hard pencil draw carefully over every line of the pattern. When tracing paper is lifted, you will find the design transferred in clear chalky outline.

PREPARING THE SURFACE

The surface on which the gold-leaf design is to be placed must be free of moisture or stickiness. Dust with a dry lintless cloth. Do not use a tack cloth; even the slight residue from this might cause blurs of unwanted gold to remain on the background. A bright sunny day helps keep a dry surface for working. Some decorators increase surface dryness by dusting with Bon Ami powder or talcum. The important thing is that the surface be clean and dry.

APPLYING THE SIZE

1. Using a pointed sable brush, paint the transferred design, taking care to stay carefully within the lines.

a. For painting, mix a small amount of medium yellow or red Japan paint in a large bottle cap with a tablespoon or so of varnish size. (See paragraph on sizing in this chapter.)

b. If it is a large design, paint only 4 or 5 inches at a time, spreading the paint-mixture very thin and working from the center toward the edge. This prevents ridges of size from setting around rim of design. Scrolls, tendrils, and other fine lines should be painted last, since they dry faster and reach the stage of being ready for the gold-leaf more quickly. Exert great care to avoid smudging the background, as gold-leaf will adhere to any surface which is at all sticky.

TESTING THE SURFACE

As you work, go back and test with the fingertip the size that has been applied to the first units of the pattern. The right stage is reached when there is just the slightest pull of adhesiveness in the size, similar to the tacky stage in bronze stenciling. When the size is somewhat dry or "siccative" it is ready for application of the leaf. Old timers call this moment the "right tack."

APPLYING THE GOLD-LEAF

1. From the book of gold-leaf, cut a piece just slightly larger than the unit of the design you wish to cover. (It is presumed that you are using gold-leaf backed on one side with tissue and on the other with waxed paper. The procedure is the same in any case.) If your gold-leaf is backed on only one side, to facilitate handling, cut a piece of waxed paper exactly the same size and place it on the exposed leaf.

2. Pick up the leaf by placing the finger tips in contact with the waxed-paper backing. Warmth of fingers will permit lifting of leaf.

3. Gently remove the other piece of tissue so as to expose the gold-leaf.

4. Place the gold-leaf on the moist varnished surface, and gently rub the waxed paper with cotton until the leaf has completely adhered to the size.

5. Remove the waxed paper.

6. Use a dry brush to push flecks of leaf lying outside design area into place on the tacky varnish.

7. Continue applying the leaf over remainder of design, and allow to dry for 24 hours or longer.

8. When work is completely dry and all raw edges of leaf have been wiped off the design, apply a protective coat of thin varnish to the entire design area. Better wait 2 or 3 days before applying the varnish coat to insure dryness all the way through to base of design.

CORRECTING MISTAKES

If gold-leaf sticks in unwanted places outside the design-area, try to remove it with carbon tetrachloride or superfine steel wool. If you seem to be marring the background coat, go over the damaged area with some of the same paint you applied for the background.

Use a fine pointed sable brush and the original background paint to make a better line on any part of the design which needs correcting, such as a ragged scroll or uneven edge.

It is always wise to reserve some background paint for such purposes.

OTHER TECHNIQUES

TRACING AND TRANSFERRING DESIGNS

Patterns may be taken from many sources by means of tracings which you can make on regular artists tracing-paper. A large pad of this may be bought from an art-supply store.

There is no need to limit your pattern-collecting to antique designs from chairs, trays, or boxes. Into your pattern scrapbook should go scrolls, bird and flower sketches from such unlikely places as china cups, seed catalogues, or flower and fruit prints. I once found an excellent scroll pattern on a gilt-painted radiator! Flowers from seed catalogues may be traced and, with a little ingenuity, redrawn with petals, leaves, and stamens separated to form a stencil pattern. It is this manipulation of borrowed material which provides fun and stimulation to the amateur-decorator.

STEP-BY-STEP DIRECTIONS

1. Place tracing paper over the pattern and draw it carefully, using a medium-hard pencil.

2. To transfer it, cover the back of the tracing-paper with white powder, either rubbed on with plain white chalk or with lithopone-powder from an art-supply store. Lithopone-powder is preferable; rub it into the tracing paper evenly with a piece of cotton. For a light background, blacken back of pattern with soft lead pencil or use graphite paper.

3. Place the tracing paper, chalked side down, on the design surface. Using a hard pencil, draw over the pattern, being careful to outline every part of it. Take care to hold the pattern firmly in place with one hand. If it is a large design, anchor it with masking tape. Masking tape may be bought in rolls at most hardware or art-supply stores. It is a light-weight paper tape, easily removed after the design is transferred.

There are several ways of making a pattern fit the size of your special project. The most painless way is to take the pattern to a photostat shop and have a blueprint of your design made in the exact size needed. This service is available in all large cities and usually costs under a dollar. In places where there is no blueprint service, the enlarging or reducing of patterns may be done at home.

To Enlarge a Pattern

1. Draw a rectangle around the outside of the original pattern. Divide it into 1-inch squares.

2. Measure the space in which you plan to use the enlarged design, and line it off in the same number of squares. The squares will of course be larger than the ones on the original design. With these lines as guide, simply draw the pattern in the larger squares, using the smaller drawing as a key.

To Reduce a Pattern

1. Reverse the squared-paper method for enlarging patterns. Make your second drawing with smaller squares. No matter what its size, the number of horizontal and vertical lines must be exactly the same as in your first drawing. When the rectangle is squared off, draw the design, using the lines as a guide.

To Center a Pattern

An easy way to be certain a pattern is in the correct position is to place a small pencil mark in the center of the chair-slat. Cut both carbon paper and tracing paper to fit the slat, and make a small hole in the center of both carbon and tracing. Move the carbon and tracing paper about on the slat until the pencil mark appears in the small hole.

PLATE 1. Six American chairs in natural wood.

PART II

Historical Notes and Working Designs

7

American Painted Chairs

ANTIQUE dealers sometimes remark that Early American chairs were painted to disguise mismatched wood. Windsor chairs often had soft pine seats with legs, spindles, and side posts of hard wood. Perhaps these chairs were painted for utility's sake. Windsors in the original dark green or black, with yellow striping as the only ornamentation, are becoming increasingly rare, but there are still enough of them to be found to indicate that few, if any, were left with a natural-wood finish. It is the present-day vogue for hand-rubbed pine and maple that has caused many of the old chairs to be stripped of their paint.

WINDSOR CHAIRS

Many Windsor chairs which have the original dark coat of paint are in such poor condition that an owner need have no qualms about scraping down and refinishing them in natural wood. However, to scrape away the design and decoration willfully on the few remaining painted Sheraton or Hepplewhite chairs or even the American fancy chairs is a different matter altogether. My advice is, if you own one of these treasures, keep it as it is! It will be a much more valuable antique twenty-five years from now if you do not tamper with the original decoration in any way. If it is dingy, wash it clean with warm water and mild soapsuds and then give the whole chair a coat of clear varnish to preserve it.

These chairs, a few of which remain in their original colors after a hundred and fifty years, are rare and interesting, and the grace of the decoration seems to me convincing evidence that they were painted for beauty alone rather than to cover unmatched woods. They were doubtless designed for the homes in London which were planned by the Adam brothers, famed interior decorators between 1785 and 1800. These two men, who were responsible for the classic revival in England, created gracious interiors which were enhanced by light-painted furniture. Many chairs were in white, aqua-green, or blue, and were exquisitely decorated with roses, urns, flowers, and birds in natural colors. As dining chairs with upholstered seats or as side chairs for an Adam drawing room, they must have been very charming.

AMERICAN HEPPLEWHITE

A fine example of American Hepplewhite is illustrated on Plate 2. It may be seen in the Metropolitan Museum of Art in New York. Made in Philadelphia in 1796, the overall color is oyster-white. The plumes which form the back slat are a delicately shaded blue-green. Moss-rosebuds and leaves decorate the toprail, and gold-leaf acanthus leaves at the base of the side post give elegance. This is no cover-up of mismatched woods! The enhancement of the delicate architecture of the piece seems to have been the sole purpose of the designer. This chair was undoubtedly made from cartoons of one of the great cabinetmakers.

Sheraton, as well as Hepplewhite, designed painted chairs, and Sheraton's *Cabinet-Maker and Upholsterer's Drawing-Book*, published about 1800 in England, was widely used as pattern book and guide by chairmakers in America. This book gives careful directions for achieving the greenish-blue of so many of the chairs of Sheraton. He recommends painting rush seats gray or white, but this finish has not proved so durable a finish for rush as varnish.

PLATE 2. American-made Hepplewhite chair, dated 1796.
Courtesy Metropolitan Museum of Art, New York City

PLATE 3. American-made Hepplewhite chair, circa 1796.
Courtesy Metropolitan Museum of Art, New York City

AMERICAN SHERATON

Many American Sheraton chairs were painted to represent more elaborate woods or burled veneers and were called "fancy chairs." Thus a plain solid-maple chair was sometimes painted with brown whorls and swirls to imitate bird's-eye or curly maple. On this painted finish a design was often applied in bronze painting and gold-leaf. Fine black-etched lines appeared in the gold-leaf to point up the design. An example of this type of chair appears in Plate 6. Pattern 1 shows how to reproduce this fine example of bronze painting.

Some Sheraton fancy chairs were painted black with formal Greek decorations in gold. Fine yellow striping accented the architectural lines. It has been said that Sheraton's designs were ruined when he came under the influence of Empire styles. Be that as it may, these gold-and-black chairs look very attractive in modern living rooms.

[49]

PLATE 4. Sheraton fancy chair. Background is yellow and design is in naturalistic greens and reddish brown.
Courtesy Essex Institute, Salem, Mass.

Early Sheraton Fancy Chair

THIS CHAIR, *circa* 1810, is made of curly maple and decorated with a handsome design in bronze painting. The scrolls and plumes are etched with fine black pen lines and the structural details of the chair are pointed up with striping in coach-yellow and black. If you are planning to decorate a similar chair, paint it black, dark green, or dark brown, since the gold scroll-design is more effective when rendered on a dark ground than on curly maple. When you have selected your color, read again the section in Chapter 2 on Preparing Chairs for Decorating.

STEP-BY-STEP DIRECTIONS

TRACING THE DESIGN

1. Fold a piece of strong transparent tracing paper in half. Unfold and trace Fig. 3 on one side of the crease, flush with the crease.

2. Only half the pattern is shown in Fig. 3. To complete pattern, refold the tracing paper, with the front of the tracing on the inside. Within the fold, place a piece of graphite paper facing the blank half of the tracing paper. Draw over the design as it shows through the back of the tracing paper. The finished design should look like Fig. 1.

3. Sprinkle lithopone-powder on back of tracing and spread powder evenly with piece of cotton.

4. Place the chair on a table with the top-slat facing you.

5. Place the traced design in position on the top-slat, powdered side down.

6. Draw entire outline of the design and lift tracing paper carefully. The pattern should appear on the chair in white outline. You are now ready to paint it in bronze.

APPLYING THE DESIGN

1. Mix Rich Gold Powder with 2 teaspoons spar-varnish until it has the consistency of cream.

2. Use a No. 3 pointed sable brush and paint the design by following the outline of the tracing.

Note: An alternate method is to mix yellow ochre or vermilion tube-paint with the varnish and paint over the transferred design in this color. Allow the scroll to become almost dry, so that it seems tacky but not too sticky to the touch. Then rub gold powder over the entire design with either a dry brush or the "velvet finger" used for stenciling. (See Chapter 5, on Stenciling.) Either method may be followed successfully, but it is slightly easier to paint fine scrolls with a color than with bronze-powder, as bronze in varnish tends to spread.

3. After the design is thoroughly dry, draw in the thin lines with a pen, as indicated in the pattern. For this work use a crow-quill, or other fine drawing pen, and Higgins permanent black drawing ink.

4. Trace Fig. 4, which is half of the middle-slat design, and complete tracing as you did with Fig. 3. This decoration is equally effective on a straight horizontal slat, if your chair has that.

5. Apply decoration to the middle-slat by the same method used for the top-slat, finishing with shading in pen strokes as in Fig. 2. (Fig. 2 is the complete drawing of the middle-slat.)

6. Apply striping to margins, as indicated in the pattern. The narrow inner stripe is the standard yellow-striping color. The wide stripes are applied in bronze powder. See Chapter 4, section on Striping, for full directions.

PLATE 6. Sheraton fancy chair, circa 1815, of Birdseye and curly maple with decoration in painted bronze and etched gold-leaf. See Pattern 1.

Owned by Dr. Pauline Dederer, Connecticut College for Women.

PLATE 7. Sheraton fancy chair, circa 1810. Made for famous Crowninshield Yacht, *Cleopatra's Barge.*

Courtesy Essex Institute, Salem, Mass.

PLATE 8. Sheraton fancy chair, circa 1815. The Medallion insert in back-slat is of similar construction to those seen on late Windsor chairs. (See Plate 14.)

Courtesy Essex Institute, Salem, Mass.

PLATE 9. Sheraton fancy chair, circa 1815, with rare latticed middle slat.

Owned by the author.

Note: Where a wide stripe runs to the outer edge of the slat, as in this design, use masking tape to keep the inner line even. Apply tape at inner side of wide stripe, cutting curved corners from the tape as indicated in pattern. Apply stripe, allow to dry, and remove tape.

FINISHING

Read Chapter 3, section on Final Finishing, and complete chair as directed there.

Fancy chair on which Pattern 1 would be appropriate

PATTERN 1. EARLY SHERATON FANCY CHAIR (*See Plate* 6.)

Fig. 1: Complete design for top-slat. Do not trace. *Fig. 3:* Pattern for one-half of top-slat. Do not trace shading lines. These are a guide for drawing pen lines.

Fig. 2: Complete design for middle-slat. Do not trace. *Fig. 4:* Pattern for one-half of middle-slat. Do not trace shading lines. These are used as guide for drawing pen-line shading. *Fig. 5:* Suggested striping plan for front of seat. Do not trace. This is only a guide.

Late-Type Fancy Chair

THE STENCILED fancy chair shown in Plate 10 is a fine example of the later type with stenciling instead of bronze painting for decoration. It was probably made no later than 1825, but it is a forerunner of the stenciled Hitchcocks. There is a suggestion of the famous Hitchcock patterns, especially in the border design. The pattern is also reminiscent of the famous honeysuckle design used on bronze-painted fancy chairs and on empire side chairs.

The original of this chair is painted black with a simple gold-powder decoration. It would be suitable, if you preferred, in barn-red, dark green or blue as background. I have also seen chairs of almost identical construction painted golden brown, and mottled and grained to simulate curly or bird's eye maple.

STEP-BY-STEP DIRECTIONS

BACKGROUND

(Refer to Chapter 2, Preparing Chairs for Decorating.) Give two coats of flat or enamel-undercoat paint in the color of your choice. Do not use enamel as it has too high a gloss. Allow chair to dry.

CUTTING THE STENCIL

(Refer to Chapter 5, section on Cutting the Stencil.)

1. Trace Figs. 1, 3a, 4, 5, 6, and 7 on separate pieces of architects-linen, leaving a ¾-inch margin of linen around each drawing. Carefully cut these stencils and number each one.

2. Cut Fig. 2 and Fig. 2a on the same piece of stencil-linen for convenience in handling.

APPLYING THE STENCILS

(Refer to chapter 5, section on Applying Stencils.)

1. Place the chair on a rather low table with top back-slat facing you.

2. Give this main back-slat and the front curve of the seat a coat of thin varnish. Allow to dry to the tacky stage.

3. Apply the central-rosette pattern, Fig. 2a, in Pale Gold Powder to exact center of top back-slat.

4. Carefully remove stencil to avoid spilling gold-dust.

5. Stencil Fig. 2 over Fig. 2a, working powder from outside edge toward center. Use Rich Gold Powder.

6. Apply Fig. 1 in Rich Gold, first to the left side of the back-slat. Clean stencil with carbon tetrachloride.

7. Reverse stencil, and apply to right side of top-slat. Refer to photograph, Plate 10, to check actual placing of stencils.

8. Turn chair so that the flat molding at the front of the seat is in a good working position.

9. Apply in Pale Gold, center motif, Fig. 7. Use a tape measure very gingerly against the tacky varnished surface to determine the center.

10. Stencil chair-front motif, Fig. 6, in Rich Gold, on left side of seat-rail, placing the side marked "end" at extreme end.

11. Clean stencil and turn it over.

12. Apply the same design to the right side of front of chair. (Refer to photograph, Plate 10.)

13. Take stencil cutting of Fig. 5 in Rich Gold and apply to each arm of chair, allowing the design to come well over curve of arm-rail.

14. Apply stencil cutting of Fig. 3a to each side-

post of chair, with the part marked "finial" at the very top of the post.

(Fig. 4, which in the original chair was applied to both side-posts, under the arms, is not really necessary. You may use it if you like, but I like the chair just as much with a plain section under the arm. The use of Fig. 4 makes the chair somewhat overdecorated.)

FINISHING AND STRIPING

(Refer to Chapter 3, Background Finishes; also to section in Chapter 4 on Striping.)

1. When chair is dry, wipe over all stenciling with a damp cloth to remove excess gold powder. Allow to dry thoroughly.

2. If the finish seems smooth to the touch, apply only one coat of satin-varnish for a finish.

3. If the surface seems rough, rub down with 4/0 steel wool; then apply a thin coat of spar-varnish.

4. When dry, rub down with powdered pumice and water. Clean off excess pumice with damp cloth. Allow to dry.

5. Apply a second and final coat of satin-varnish.

PLATE 10. Pattern 2. Late stenciled fancy chair, circa 1825.
Owned by Mrs. Robert Cummins, Winchester, Mass.

[57]

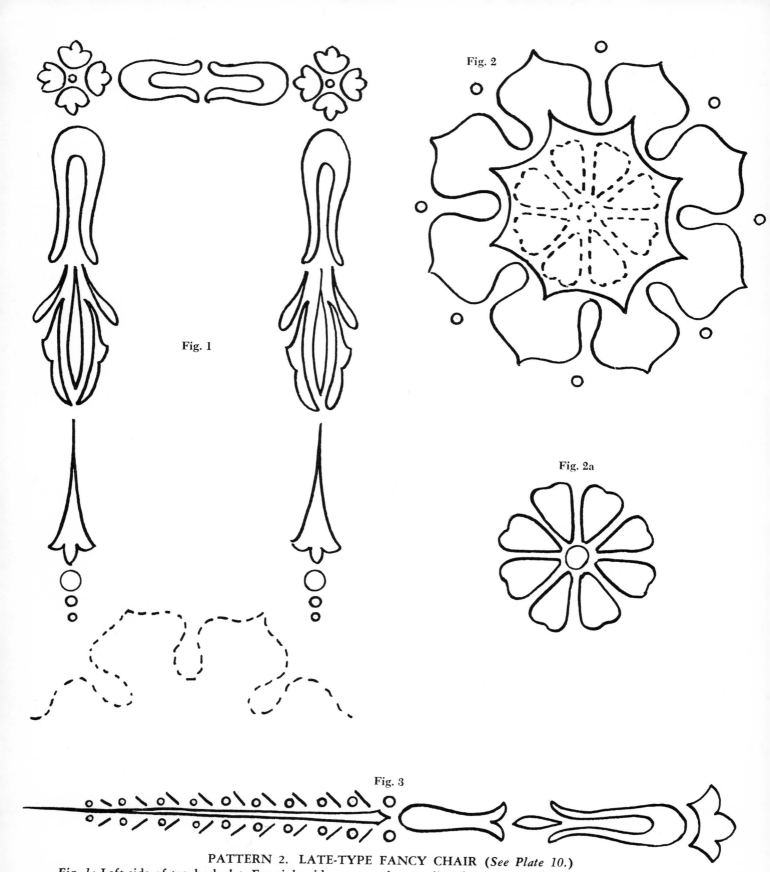

PATTERN 2. LATE-TYPE FANCY CHAIR (*See Plate 10.*)

Fig. 1: Left side of top back-slat. For right side, reverse the stencil and, when transferring the design, place to right of central rosette. *Fig. 2:* Rosette, the central motif of top back-slat. *Fig. 2a:* Central portion of large rosette. *Fig. 3:* Motif for side-post.

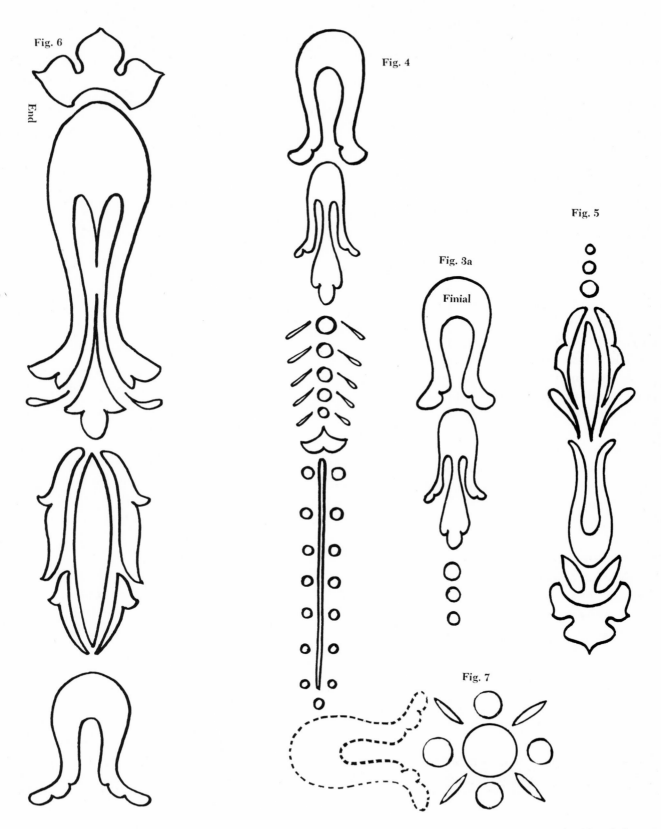

Fig. 3a: Motif for side-post (top). *Fig. 4:* Side-post, under arm. *Fig. 5:* Arm of chair. *Fig. 6:* **Left side of front of chair seat.** Reverse Stencil to apply pattern to right side. *Fig. 7:* Motif for center front of chair seat.

[59]

8

Country Windsors

THE straight wooden-seated chair known by various names—thumb-back, arrow-back or Sheraton Windsor—is most often seen today in a natural rubbed-maple finish. The soft pine seats are finished to match the harder maple or fruit-wood legs, slats, and posts. After closely examining this type of chair in various houses in Deerfield, Massachusetts, I have come to the conclusion that most of these chairs originally were painted and not left in the natural-wood finish. Observations of this type of simple handmade chair throughout Pennsylvania corroborate the opinion that few chairs were left unpainted. It is doubtless true that paint was applied because several different woods were used in the same chair and painting concealed the mismatching.

Poplar and hickory were almost as prevalent as maple and pine. Colors vary in different parts of the country. Dark green and rusty black with yellow striping were especially popular in Vermont, New York, and western Massachusetts; while Maine, eastern Massachusetts, Rhode Island, and Connecticut seem to have had more dark brown and country-yellow chairs. A number of yellow chairs seem to have originated in New Jersey and Maryland, too. In Pennsylvania, bright greens, blues, and browns were common; but by far the most popular color seems to have been red; even today more red chairs in their original paint turn up in Pennsylvania than anywhere else. This Venetian-red background color may be duplicated today by buying barn-red or Venetian red and toning it

down with a small amount of raw umber in tube oil-paint.

The placing of colors geographically is admittedly pure guesswork, as it is impossible to make an accurate check when probably eighty per cent of the antique chairs have been scraped clean of the cracking paint and rubbed down.

This popular straight chair was used both as a kitchen and a dining chair, when "dining" took place mostly around a drop-leaf table in a great homey kitchen. It was decorated most often with a simple striping on the dark paint, possibly a running-leaf pattern on the arrow-shaped spindles. Sometimes the top-slat had in the center a small oval painted with a landscape, and delicate scrolls on either side. (See Plate 13.) When the top-slat was decorated, we often find simple, round spindles forming the back rather than flat or arrow-spindles.

Another popular decoration for these wooden chairs was the rose motif, either stylized or in a naturalistic rendering. There are countless variations of the rose motif in chair decoration. The calla lily was also popular, and I have seen a set of twelve painted chairs, still in fine condition, with a different garden flower on each. Among the flowers on this fascinating set are the fuchsia, pansy, lily-of-the-valley, cyclamen, moss rose, and forget-me-not. It is as if the maker had gone to his flower garden and recorded the plants growing there.

PLATE 11. Common Yellow chair, circa 1830. This rare example of original stenciling and brush-stroke painting has not been retouched.
Owned by the author.

PLATE 12. Half arrow-back chair with **bamboo** turnings, circa 1825. Original stencil design in mint condition. Note similarity to the cross-piece design on early Hitchcock chair, Plate. 19.

PLATE 13. Landscape medallion chair, circa 1820. Pattern 3. A type often referred to as Sheraton Windsor, because of a similarity to both the Sheraton and the Windsor styles.
Owned by Mrs. Robert Cummins, Winchester, Mass.

PLATE 14. Windsor arm chair with medallion insert in top-piece. Design executed in brush-stroke painting. The design panel is held in place by being pierced through the back by the central spindle, which extends through it to the top-rail.
Owned by Dr. Pauline Dederer, Connecticut College for Women.

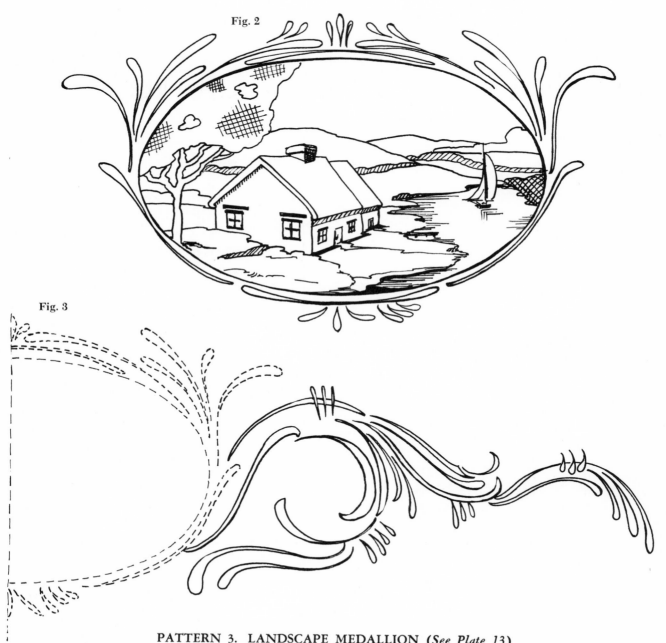

PATTERN 3. LANDSCAPE MEDALLION (*See Plate 13*)

Fig. 1: Miniature drawing of top-slat. (To be used only for reference.) *Fig. 2:* Landscape medallion, central motif. *Fig. 3:* Scroll for right side. For left side, reverse tracing to complete pattern.

Landscape Medallion Chair

THE original chair from which this pattern was derived is painted black with the landscape in naturalistic coloring and the scrolls in oyster-white. The scene might well be a Vermont farm, since the chair had been in the family of a Vermont farmer for many years and is similar in its construction to the Country Windsors made in Vermont and New Hampshire. Today a sketch of some familiar scene, made perhaps from a snapshot, would give a personal touch to such a chair and make it uniquely your own. It is a simple pattern and might be classed with "easy-to-make" dresses in the style books. (Refer to Plate 13.) .

STEP-BY-STEP DIRECTIONS

BACKGROUND

(Refer to Chapter 2, Preparing Chairs for Decorating, and Chapter 3, Background Finishes.)

1. Paint background in color of your choice.

2. On a dark background, apply to the oval which contains the landscape one or two coats of white enamel-undercoat to make an opaque backing for the landscape colors. Allow oval to become thoroughly dry.

TRANSFERRING THE PATTERN

1. Select a piece of tracing-paper about an inch larger all around than top-slat of chair and fold in half to find center.

2. Place center crease over center of medallion in Fig. 2, and trace.

3. Fit tracing over dotted lines in Fig. 3, and trace scroll.

4. Fold tracing paper in center and complete scroll on left side of medallion by tracing right scroll in reverse. You should now have a tracing of the complete design for top-slat.

5. To transfer design, cover back of tracing with lithopone-powder for work on a dark background. Use charcoal powder if background is light.

6. Rub back of area of tracing containing landscape with a charcoal pencil in any case, since it is to be transferred to the light oval of the landscape.

7. Place tracing in position on top-slat of chair, powder side down, and draw over pattern. When you remove tracing, a line-drawing of pattern should remain on chair. Placing the chair in a horizontal position on a work table is a help in accomplishing this work efficiently.

PREPARING FOR PAINTING

1. Colors needed: Prussian blue, permanent green, chrome-yellow medium, alizarin crimson, Titanium or Philips White, mauve, and lamp-black.

2. Mix equal quantities of turpentine and spar-varnish as a medium for use with artists-oils in painting landscape and scrolls.

PAINTING THE LANDSCAPE

1. Do the *sky* first, using Prussian blue with a speck of alizarin to tone it down. The area at the top of the sky should be comparatively dark. Mix the paint so thin in turpentine and varnish that it is transparent.

2. Add white and a speck of yellow to lighten it as you paint down to the line of the mountain. The white should show through clearly as you come to the horizon, the sky at the back of the mountains being almost as light as the white background.

3. Paint the *water,* using the light blue remaining in your brush after doing the sky. Paint the

whole area of the lake in this color.

4. Paint the *shadows* at the shore line of the lake, adding more Prussian blue toned down with black and a tiny bit of mauve and alizarin crimson. (In the pattern, shadow areas are marked with horizontal lines.) Let the shadows fade into the light color in the center of the lake.

5. Paint over the light blue in center of lake, using a transparent glaze of Prussian blue.

6. Paint the *roof* of the house brown with burnt sienna.

7. Outline the *windows* in brown.

8. Outline the *main structural lines* of the house in black.

9. Paint the *body of the house* white.

10. Paint the *mountains* in Prussian blue mixed with permanent green and a little black. Let lightest tone come at the top and darken toward the line of bushes that cuts across the center of the picture with vertical lines.

11. Paint the *bushes* yellow-green, for which you add chrome yellow or yellow ochre and white to permanent green.

12. Paint the *grass* in the left foreground permanent green slightly darkened by adding alizarin and Prussian blue. (The grass should not be nearly so dark as the shadows of the water which lie next to it.)

13. Paint the *trees* the color of the grass, with

the crisscross sections a deeper green to indicate shadows. (In some of the landscapes on old furniture the right-hand side of trees, houses, bushes, and other objects was outlined in burnt sienna to avoid a flat effect. This is rather quaint, so try it if you like.)

SCROLLS AND STRIPING

1. If the background of chair is dark, paint *scrolls and striping* in oyster-white or yellow. (Oyster-white is made by mixing small amounts of mauve and chrome yellow with white—just enough to make it an "off white.")

2. If background is light, use a deep blue-green for *scrolls and striping*. Mix Prussian blue, chrome-yellow medium, white, and black until you have a satisfactory dark aqua color.

(It is difficult to paint scrolls with any freedom of movement unless you practice the brush stroke first. Try the scroll on a piece of cardboard which has been primed with a coat of paint before working on the chair.)

3. *Striping*. (Read Chapter 4, section on Striping.)

Mix all striping colors with clear varnish only. Do not add turpentine.

FINISHING

(Read Chapter 3, section on Final Finishing.) Complete chair according to directions.

Medallion appropriate for country Windsor chair

Pennsylvania Country Chair

THIS pattern is from a Pennsylvania country chair, probably made between 1830 and 1840. I am including it because it is simple and sturdy and its prototype may be seen in many homes today. It is well suited to the amateur decorator since the original pattern was first set by means of a stencil, and was then freely over-painted, leaving in gold only a metallic border and the highlights on fruits and tips of leaves. The background color is a dark apple-green. Dark blue, black, or barn-red could be used for the background with equal authenticity.

STEP-BY-STEP DIRECTIONS
CUTTING THE STENCIL

1. Measure the top back-slat of the chair and cut a piece of architects-linen half an inch larger on all four sides.

2. Measure the middle-slat and cut another piece of architects-linen, also with the half-inch margin.

3. Trace pattern of top-slat from drawing Fig. 1 and Fig. 1a on dull side of linen. Fit Fig. 1a into Fig. 1 as you make the drawing. The two parts should be joined as in a jig-saw puzzle for your completed tracing.

4. Cut stencil so that, when finished, the pattern for the top-slat will be one continuous design. (Fig. 3.)

5. Trace pattern of middle-slat by combining Fig. 2 and Fig. 2a. First trace Fig. 2. Then place dotted line over dotted line on Fig. 2a, and trace.

6. Complete pattern by turning stencil-linen over, matching up dotted lines and tracing Fig. 2. You will now find yourself tracing Fig. 2 on the glossy side of linen.

7. Retrace this section of Fig. 2 so that completed tracing will show entire pattern on dull side of linen.

8. Cut stencil for middle-slat. The border holes may be made with a commercial punch. Sometimes an inexpensive hand-punch from a stationery store will cut a neat clean hole. (This method of making the holes saves an inestimable amount of time.)

STENCILING THE PATTERN

(Read Chapter 5, sections Varnishing before Stenciling and Applying Bronze Powders.)

1. Place chair in horizontal position on work table.

2. Wipe middle-slat clean with tack cloth and apply a thin coat of varnish. Allow to dry until tacky.

3. Adjust combined stencil of Figs. 2 and 2a so that it is in center of slat. Holding it firmly in place with left hand, apply the bronze powders. (Stencil may be anchored in place with masking tape if you do not trust the steadying power of your left hand.)

4. Stencil *leaves* and *center section of escutcheon* in Brushed Brass Powder.

5. Stencil *flowers, dots,* and *border lines* in Aluminum Powder.

6. Wipe top-slat with tack cloth and apply a thin coat of varnish. Allow to dry until tacky.

7. Place stencil of Figs. 1 and 1a in position and apply bronze powders.

    a. Stencil *large fruits* and *leaves* in Brushed Brass.

PLATE 15. Pennsylvania chair back, circa 1850. Two-slat chair restored by the author from an original chair in Plymouth Meeting, Pennsylvania.

PLATE 16. Stenciled arrow-back chair. Design over-painted in natural colors. Dark reddish brown background. Striping: narrow stripes, authentic coach yellow; wide stripes, apple green.
Owned by Mrs. Robert Cummins, Winchester, Mass.

b. Stencil *flower, grapes,* and *border* in Aluminum Powder.

8. For high lights, work from outside edge of cut-outs toward center. Accent a high light on each *fruit,* and let bronze powder blur off on shadow side. On *leaves,* accent one side of central vein with a high light.

COLORING THE STENCIL

This old pattern was rendered with an opaque overlay instead of the usual transparent color glaze.

1. Pour 2 tablespoons spar-varnish and 1 tablespoon turpentine into a large bottle cap and stir until blended.

2. Squeeze out small quantities of English vermilion (or cadmium red), alizarin, and Titanium White on an old plate or palette. Mix colors with enough varnish and turpentine to flow easily.

3. Paint the *large fruits,* each piece separately.

4. Before paint dries, wipe out a high light at top left of each *peach* using your thumb or a dry brush. Rub all the way through to gold paint, allowing the gold to become the high light.

5. Add a blurred shadow at lower right side of *peach* by painting the still-wet surface with a dark tone of alizarin. Add a little raw umber and mauve for shadow tone. Let shadow follow rounded contour of fruit.

6. Mix ultramarine blue and mauve with varnish and paint each grape in cluster.

7. Wipe out a high light at top left of each *grape* so that silver base shows through.

8. Working fast before paint dries, deepen shadow at lower right of each *grape* by adding more mauve to blue.

9. Paint *leaves* in permanent green, lightened with Titanium White, and subdued with a bit of lamp-black.

10. Wipe out a portion of upper half of each *leaf* to suggest a high light.

11. If with all this thumb-painting you find that you have gone outside the lines of the stencil, repair the damage by repainting the immediate background with the original background color.

12. Paint *flowers* in middle-slat with alizarin and

English vermilion mixture used for peaches. Suggest shadow at lower right of flowers with deeper tone. Leaves are painted in exactly the same way as on top-slat.

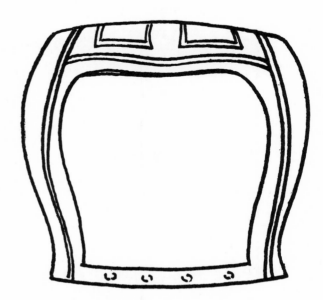

Chart of striping—Pennsylvania chair

STRIPING

(Read Chapter 4, section on Striping, for complete directions and color formulas. Refer to Drawing, for placing of striping on seat.)

1. Paint *fine stripes* on side-posts in yellow:

2. Paint *wide stripes* in green.

3. Paint *knobs* and *turnings* with Brushed Brass Powder.

4. Varnish knob half-way around. Allow varnish to dry to tacky stage.

5. Apply gold powder.

FINISHING

(Read Chapter 3, Final Finishing.) Complete chair according to directions there.

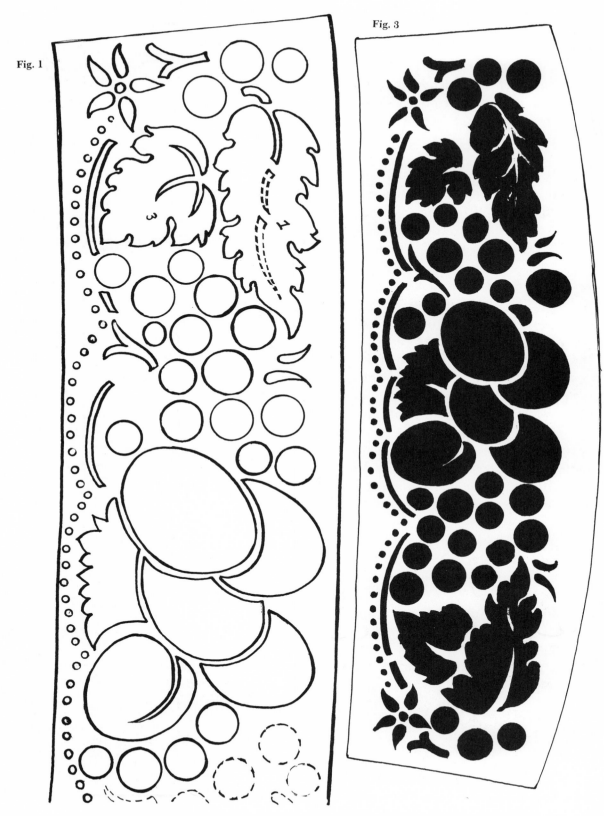

Fig. 1

Fig. 3

PATTERN 4. PENNSYLVANIA COUNTRY CHAIR (*See Plate 15.*)

Fig. 1: Part of top-slat. This is to be fitted together with *Fig. 1a* on following page to make complete top-slat pattern.
Fig. 3: Complete top-slat. Do not trace. This is a guide.

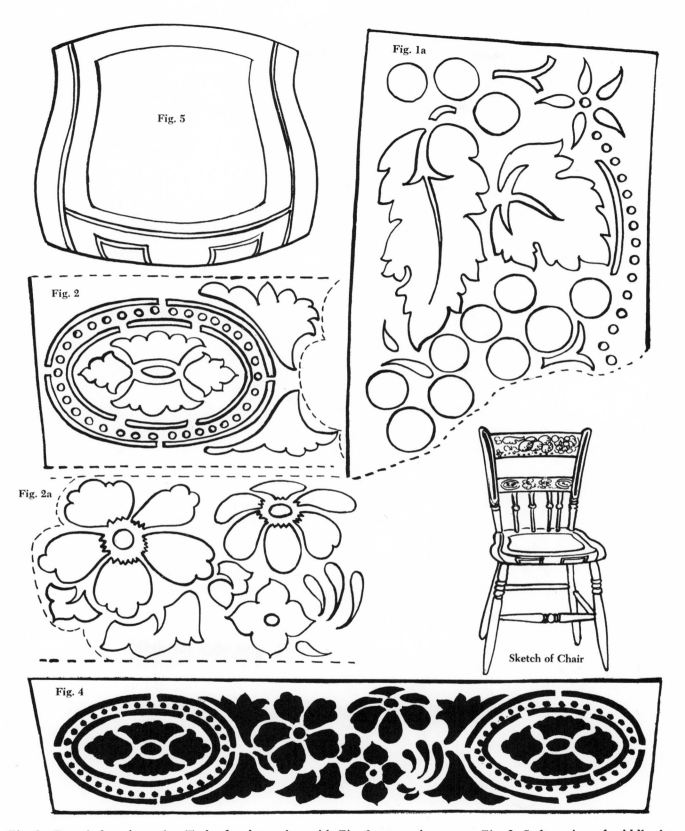

Fig. 1a: Remainder of top-slat. To be fitted together with *Fig. 1* on previous page. *Fig. 2:* Left section of middle-slat. Reverse for right section. *Fig. 2a:* Center of middle-slat. To be fitted against dotted lines of *Fig. 2. Fig. 4:* Sketch of middle-slat. Do not trace. This is a guide. *Fig. 5:* Guide sketch of striping for seat.

PLATE 17. Plank-bottom stenciled chair in the Hitchcock style. Made by John Hull in 1838. *Courtesy American Index of Design, National Gallery, Washington, D. C.*

9

Hitchcock Chairs

THE name "Hitchcock," as applied to a chair, has come to mean a certain type with cane or rush-bottom seat, turned legs, and a wide, slightly-curved, horizontal slat which forms the back. These chairs are painted black or finished with an imitation grain to represent mahogany, walnut, or rosewood, and are decorated with elaborate designs in bronze stenciling. Many of them have two somewhat narrow back-slats instead of one wide one.

Lambert Hitchcock, the man who gave his name to the chair, was born in Cheshire, Connecticut, in 1795 and died in 1852. He was one of the few furniture men who signed his wares and, because of this stencil "Lambert Hitchcock, Warranted," which was stamped on the back of the many chairs made in his factory, the so-called Hitchcock chair has become famous. Other men had made such chairs, at least ten and possibly twenty years earlier than Hitchcock, but because he signed them, the name of Hitchcock remains to this day.

He founded a thriving factory at Hitchcocksville, Connecticut, and made many kinds of chairs there. The most typical is shaped like the drawing.

The three other sketches show shapes which were produced at this famous factory and have as much right to be called Hitchcocks as the better-known variety.

HITCHCOCK SIGNATURES

There are three distinct forms of signature. From 1828 until 1832 it was: "L. Hitchcock, Hitchcocksville, Connecticut Warranted." After 1832, when he had taken his brother-in-law into partnership, the stenciled signature read, "Hitchcock Alford & Co., Warranted." In 1840 Hitchcock moved to Unionville, Connecticut, and opened a factory there. Chairs made there are marked "Lambert Hitchcock, Unionville, Connecticut." There are some chairs to be found today made by Hitchcock's brother-in-law after Lambert left the firm. These bear the name of "Alford and Company" and were probably manufactured between 1840 and 1860.

A study of the life of Lambert Hitchcock reads like a novel, for he was a young man with a dream. He had ideas for assembly-line techniques and merchandising far in advance of his day. If transportation had been easier, his Connecticut-made chairs would have been marketed in quantity-shipments to the North, South, and West. Shipping difficulties in the 1820's prevented the free flow of finished products from his factory, and it was often impossible to keep supply and demand in ratio.

If Hitchcock had been able to get these chairs to more remote markets and could have collected payment in reasonable time, he would probably

Typical Hitchcock chair

have been able to avoid bankruptcy. As it was, in 1828 when, as a "consequence of repeated losses and misfortunes," he was forced to liquidate for the benefit of his creditors, he had fifteen hundred chairs in the factory at Hitchcocksville and another fifteen hundred at a wholesale dealer's in Hartford. In looking over his old ledgers, one comes across the item that a large quantity of stock for the manufacture of these chairs was in the hands of the Warden of the state's prison in Wethersfield, where Hitchcock had sent them to be assembled. It is probable that the finished chairs came back to the factory for painting and bronze stenciling.

After three years of running the factory for his creditors, Hitchcock was able to clear himself of debt. It was about this time, 1832, that he took his brother-in-law, Arba Alford, into partnership and the name, "Hitchcock Alford and Co. Warranted," began to appear on his chairs. The 1832 price seems to have been about a dollar and a half apiece, which provides an interesting comparison with present-day prices.

HITCHCOCK DESIGNS

Lambert Hitchcock probably did the designs for few if any of the chairs himself. He was a businessman rather than an artist. He employed "gilders" to stencil the famous fruit patterns on his chairs and even taught women to do the gold stenciling. There is evidence that he sent chairs out of the factory to be assembled. Journeymen cabinet-makers in nearby Massachusetts are known to have used identical stencil patterns, and it is possible that these men took chairs "knocked down" to their homes and did the art work away from the factory. They may even have completed the chairs and formed retail units for selling them, as Hitchcock used considerable ingenuity in getting his chairs to market. At the factory the gold-work was almost entirely done by women who applied the gold-powders to the wet varnish with the tips of their fingers.

Most popular of the early Hitchcock patterns was the bowl of fruit containing stylized grapes, foliage, and melons, peaches or pears. Two sprays of small flowers dripping over each side were often cut in one piece with the bowl. The fruit inside the bowl was applied in separate units. Accuracy in placing the fruits in the bowl was achieved by using a "theorem", the bowl with the side flowers

Three types of Hitchcock chair with different back treatments

Liberty symbol. Found at Dykes Mill.
Courtesy Pennsylvania Museum Bulletin.

the French liberty cap, the American eagle, also the Roman fasces appear in many stencil collections of the period.

The gilders needed to be expert in fine brushwork and clever in transferring stencil patterns. The best of the early chairs often had freehand bronze painting on the side-posts and front of the seat and fine lines of striping in bright yellow, to point up the architectural lines of the chair. Many of the early furniture gilders had been first apprenticed to carriage makers and had learned striping techniques from decorating the fine coaches of post-revolutionary times. No other painter's skill requires a steadier eye or a defter brush than striping. It is little wonder, therefore, that as the vogue for freehand bronze painting reached new heights of popularity, the logical men to do the work were coach stripers. On Hitchcock chairs the honeysuckle design on the "pillow" or "bolster" in the middle of the shoulder bar were, more often than not, done by freehand painting rather than stenciling.

HITCHCOCK FACTORY TODAY

Although Lambert Hitchcock's chair factory continued to operate long after his death, during the latter years of the nineteenth century the chairmaking industry suffered hard times. Mass production shifted to Grand Rapids, Michigan, and the Hitchcock factory changed hands many times. Even the name of the little town of Hitchcocksville, so rich in chairmaking lore, became Riverton in 1866, to avoid confusion between Hitchcocks-

acting as the axis for the design.

Later, chair-gilders used one short-cut after another to speed up working time on each chair. They came more and more to use the single-unit stencil whereby an entire pattern could be put on the back-slat of a chair in one operation. The fine bronze and silver-work achieved by careful placing of one small unit after another was lost. Delicate shadow effects were sacrificed. Thus the earlier examples of the chair-gilders craft remain superior both in execution and design to the more elaborately-cut one-unit stencils.

The "liberty" symbols used on stenciled chairs of the 1830 to 40 period are a study in themselves. The artisans of this period were intensely interested in freedom, not only in their own country but all over the world. There was great excitement here over the effort in France to gain freedom, so

Liberty stencil. Found at Dykes Mill.
Courtesy Pennsylvania Museum Bulletin.

ville and Hotchkissville. By that time the factory had been sold and chairs were no longer made there. Now, however, the fascinating old brick building has been bought by two enterprising young businessmen who have modernized and reopened it and are once more making Hitchcock chairs. This imaginative plan of constructing fine sturdy chairs on the same site where they were first made has been of great interest to all who appreciate good furniture. Many people have visited the new factory and watched every step in the making of these durable chairs.

The finished product may be bought either in natural wood to take home and decorate, or in the finest of black, mahogany, or grained-walnut finishes. The stenciling is done with an airbrush rather than by hand, which gives a slightly sharper effect, but present-day Hitchcock chairs in spite of this, are handsome indeed. The patterns and measurements of the chairs are authentic in every detail.

Famous honeysuckle or anthemium pattern

PLATE 18. Hitchcock chair, circa 1830. Fine example of built-up fruit pattern. **One of a set of four in the Edgar Rich Memorial Room of the Public Library of Winchester, Mass.**

[75]

Early Hitchcock-Type Chair

THIS two-slat chair is a transition type, so-called because it has features of the Sheraton fancy chair and of the Hitchcock. Although a turned top-rail with a bolster or pillow in the center was the most popular crest-rail on Hitchcock chairs, there were several other types that were just as certainly authentic. In the 1820s many characteristic Hitchcock chairs were made with two slats, the top-slat extending beyond the side-posts. An example of this early model is seen in Plate 19.

STEP-BY-STEP DIRECTIONS

MATERIALS

1. *For imitation-mahogany finish*
   ½ pint red background paint
   ½ pint flat-black paint
   ½ pint spar- or bar-varnish
   ox-hair varnish brush (medium size)
   2/0 sandpaper
   6/0 sandpaper (ask for wet and dry sandpaper; if possible get the new silicon carbide grit paper. It is superfine.)
   (For an all-black background omit red paint.)

2. *For applying stencils*
   ½ yard architects-linen
   scrap of silk velvet or a piece of soft chamois
   jar of Rich Gold Lining-Powder
   jar Silver or Aluminum Powder
   jar Pale Gold Powder

3. *For overpainting stencils and striping*
   2 French quill brushes ¾ inch and 1 inch long
   1 or 2 striping quill brushes
   Artist-oil tube-paints in burnt sienna, yellow ochre, chrome-yellow medium, burnt umber, raw umber, alizarin crimson

TRACING THE STENCIL

1. Place a piece of architects-linen, glossy side down, over Fig. 1, the central motif of the top-slat.

PLATE 19. Early Hitchcock chair-back, circa 1830. See Pattern 5. Note similarity in pattern on middle slat with stenciling on chair in Plate 12.
Owned by Mr. and Mrs. Edward A. Wheeler, Essex, Mass.

Leave room for an inch margin around each unit.

2. Trace Fig. 1, omitting the dotted lines.

3. Number each of the stencils.

4. Make a tracing of Fig. 2, the left side of the top-slat, directly on linen, leaving an inch margin all around.

5. Trace the *veinings* for leaves, Fig. 1a and Fig. 2a.

6. Trace Fig. 3 all in one piece. This is motif for side-post.

7. Trace Fig. 4, the motif for front of seat.

8. Make tracings of *leaf* and *fruit* units, labeled Fig. 5a, Fig. 5b, Fig. 5c, and Fig. 5d, on separate pieces of linen, leaving a margin around each.

9. Trace separately, but keep together on same piece of stencil linen, Figs. 6 and 6a, the *flower* and *stamens*.

10. Trace Fig. 1a and Fig. 2a, the *veinings* for leaves, on separate pieces of linen, always leaving the margin. (Fig. 2a is also veining for leaf Fig. 5a.)

CUTTING THE STENCIL

Fig. 7 is a reference diagram for entire design of middle-slat. (Refer to Chapter 5, section on Cutting the Stencil.)

DIRECTIONS FOR DECORATING

Prepare a low table with several layers of newspapers or a drop-cloth so that you may place the chair in a horizontal position for decorating.

1. Imitation-mahogany finish

   a. Apply a coat of red paint to chair. Allow to dry 24 hours.

   b. Apply a coat of flat-black. While paint is still wet, wipe out graining on wood with coarse cloth. (Refer to Chapter 3, section on Imitation-Rosewood Finish.)

2. Black background

   a. Apply two thin coats of flat-black paint 24 hours apart. (Read Chapter 2, section on Preparing Chairs for Decorating.)

   b. When dry, rub chair with fine sandpaper or steel wool, until finish is satin smooth.

APPLYING THE STENCILS

(Refer to Chapter 5, section on Applying the

PLATE 20. Hitchcock chair-back, 1825-1830. Imitation rosewood with designs in gold stenciling and gold-leaf. *Courtesy of Society for Preservation of New England Antiquities.*

Stencil.)

MIDDLE-SLAT

1. Place chair in horizontal position and apply thin coat of varnish to middle-slat. Allow to dry to tacky stage.

2. Place *leaf*, Fig. 5a, slightly to right of middle of slat, and apply Rich Gold Powder to *leaf*, leaving center dark.

3. Place *vein*, Fig. 2a, over shadowy dark center of leaf, and rub in Aluminum Powder.

4. Place *melon*, Fig. 5b, slightly to left of leaf, and apply Aluminum Powder to top only, allowing remainder of melon to fade off as if it were lying back of the leaf.

5. Place *peach*, Fig. 5d, just below the melon and stencil it in Pale Gold, allowing center to remain in shadow.

6. Place *flower*, Fig. 6, at upper right of leaf, and stencil outer edges, leaving center in shadow.

7. Superimpose *stamens*, Fig. 6a, on flower and rub in Aluminum Powder.

8. Make a cluster of *grapes* by stenciling Fig. 5c in several positions at lower right of central leaf.

9. Complete design by stenciling *tip of leaf,* Fig. 5a, at each end of fruit group. Allow leaf to fade off into shadow, as it comes back of the fruit.

10. When stenciling has dried thoroughly, sponge off excess bronze powder with damp cloth.

TOP-SLAT

1. Place *central leaf,* Fig. 1, in position in center of top-slat, with glossy side of stencil in contact with varnish. Rub in Rich Gold Powder. Rub only the tips of leaf, allowing center to remain in shadow.

2. Place *vein,* Fig. 1a, over center of leaf and apply Aluminum Powder.

3. Place *large leaf and scroll,* Fig. 2, in position to the left of Fig. 1 and apply Pale Gold Powder, alternating with Rich Gold.

4. For *flower and leaves at extreme end* use Rich Gold.

5. Place *vein,* Fig. 2a, over large leaf and apply Aluminum Powder.

6. Examine Plate 18 and shade stenciling accordingly.

7. Wipe off stencil Fig. 2 with Carbona to clean it.

8. Place Fig. 2 to right of *central leaf* in reverse position, thus completing pattern on top-slat. (See diagram.)

SIDE-POSTS AND FRONT OF SEAT

1. Varnish side-posts and front of seat.

2. Allow to dry to tacky stage.

3. Apply Fig. 3 to side-posts using Pale Gold Powder.

4. Apply Fig. 4 to front of seat using Pale Gold Powder. These stencils do not need to be shaded.

5. Allow to dry, then wipe off all excess powder with damp cloth.

6. When stenciling is completely dry and has been cleaned with damp cloth, give entire chair a coat of spar-varnish and allow to dry for twenty-four hours.

STRIPING

(Read Chapter 4, section on Striping.)

1. Paint all narrow stripes on this chair yellow. (Examine Plate 18 and stripe accordingly.)

2. Varnish the knob turnings on front legs and turned stretcher half way around. Allow to dry until tacky.

3. Apply gold powder.

Old chairs had gold applied only on front face of turning, never all the way around; hence in decorating old chairs, follow the same procedure.

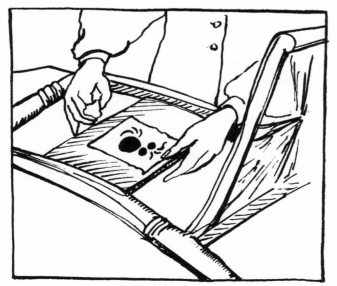

Position of chair back when stencil is applied

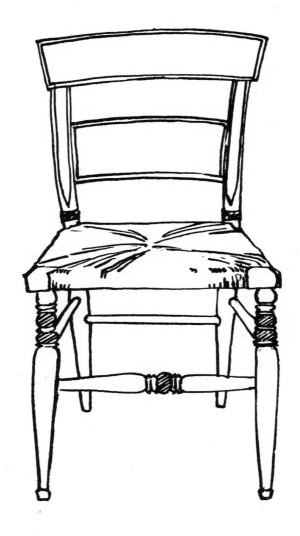

Striping chart for early Hitchcock chair

Fig. 1

Top

Complete Top-Slat

Fig. 2

Fig. 3

PATTERN 5. EARLY HITCHCOCK-TYPE CHAIR (*See Plate 19.*)

Fig. 1: Central motif of top-slat. *Fig. 2:* Left side of top-slat. Reverse for right side. (Veining for leaves on following page.) *Fig. 3:* Motif for side post.

Fig. 1a: Veining for leaf in *Fig. 1* (previous page). *Fig. 2a:* Veining for leaf in *Fig. 2. Fig. 4:* Motif for front of seat. *Fig. 5a:* Leaf in middle-slat. *Fig. 5b:* Melon in middle-slat. *Fig. 5c:* Grape in middle-slat. *Fig. 5d:* Peach in middle-slat. *Figs. 6 and 6a:* Flower in middle-slat. *Fig. 7:* Reference diagram for entire middle-slat.

Bowl-of-Fruit Design

BEFORE starting to decorate this chair (Plate 21), read the pages at the beginning of this chapter which tell the story of Lambert Hitchcock. It will renew your interest in the famous old chair which has recently had such a spectacular return to fashion. Selling for almost forty times as much as it did when it was a new furniture-style one hundred and twenty years ago, this chair is seen today in the finest contemporary shops and homes.

STEP-BY-STEP DIRECTIONS
BACKGROUND COATS

Read carefully Chapter 2, section on Preparing Chairs for Decorating, and Chapter 3, Imitation Rosewood Finish. Paint chair according to directions in the background color of your choice.

Materials needed
½ pint barn-red or vermilion paint
½ pint flat-black
½ pint spar-varnish
Medium-sized brush for background painting
Good-quality ox-hair brush for varnishing
Metallic powders for stenciling, page 37
Other materials for stenciling, page 37
Artist's transparent oils in burnt sienna, raw umber, burnt umber, chrome-yellow medium, and yellow ochre
¾-inch pointed sable brush for overpainting design
2-inch narrow quill striping brush

CUTTING THE STENCILS

1. Place a piece of architects-linen, glossy side down, directly over the bowl, Fig. 1.

2. Draw outline carefully with medium-hard pencil, leaving at least an inch margin of linen around the design.

3. Trace each unit of the design on a separate piece of linen, leaving a margin around each.

4. Number units from 1 to 10 as they are in the pattern.

5. Read Chapter 5 on Cutting the Stencil and proceed.

STENCILING THE MIDDLE-SLAT

1. Place chair on a low table with the top-rail facing you. The chair should be lying on its back.

2. Give the wide center-slat a thin coat of spar-varnish.

3. While the varnish is drying to the tacky stage, read section in Chapter 5 on Applying the Stencil.

4. Test the varnish with the tip of your finger; and when it is almost, but not quite, dry, place Fig. 1 in position, glossy side of the linen down. Hold stencil in position firmly with fingertips of left hand. Fig 1 should include the *bowl, stems of strawberries,* and *stems of grapes,* all in one cutting.

5. Dip the velvet, which you have wrapped around your finger, lightly in Pale Gold Powder and apply to the stencil. Let the right side of the bowl drift off into the shadow.

6. Stencil *stems* in silver. Do not shade stems, as they should have a sharp clear outline.

7. Carefully lift stencil from chair, taking care not to spill gold powder.

8. Place the *peach*, Fig. 7, in position and rub in Rich Gold Powder, shading it as in Plate 21.

PLATE 21. Bowl of Fruit design. See Pattern 6.
Owned by Mrs. Wayne Thompson, Winchester, Mass.

the bunch of grapes.

14. Place the *strawberry leaf,* Fig. 4, in a like manner back of the strawberries, thus building a massed foliage effect with all the leaves in Rich Gold.

This will complete stenciling of middle-slat.

SIDE-POSTS, CENTRAL SECTION OF TOP-RAIL, AND FRONT SEAT-RAIL

1. Apply a coat of varnish.
2. When varnish has reached tacky stage, apply Fig. 8 to pillow in center of top-rail, using Rich Gold Powder for stenciling.
3. An alternate and more standard motif for top-rail is Fig. 9, of which one-half is shown in pattern. Fold tracing paper in center and trace in reverse for other half, if you prefer it to Fig. 8.
4. Turn chair so the front of seat will be in good working position, and apply Fig. 8 to seat rail, using Gold. For exact position refer to Plate 21.
5. Apply Fig. 9 to extreme top of each side-post.
6. Apply Fig. 10 to rest of side-post. Refer to Plate 21 for replacing of these units.
7. Allow all stenciling to become bone dry. Then remove excess powder with a damp cloth.
8. Give entire chair a thin coat of varnish.

STRIPING

(Read section in Chapter 4 on Striping. The Hitchcock chair was usually striped in yellow.)

1. Use recipe for authentic striping yellow. See Page 34.

9. Apply the left *tip of the melon,* Fig. 6, to the left side of the peach, using silver.

10. Apply the *stem-end of the melon.* Fig. 6a, on the right side of peach, in silver.

11. Place the *strawberry,* Fig. 5, on the ends of the stems on left side of bowl. Change the position of the strawberry as you stencil, to give the effect of a cluster.

12. Assemble the bunch of *grapes* in the same way, using Fig. 3. As you stencil the grapes, place the stencil in such a way that the grapes overlap, forming a cluster. Use Silver or Aluminum Powder for the grapes. (Refer to Chapter 5, section Molding Light and Shadow.)

13. Stencil the *tip of the grape leaf,* Fig. 2, and let the leaves fade out back of the fruit bowl and

Single Leaf

Vein

Massed foliage stenciling—example of foliage made by moving a single leaf in many different positions while stenciling

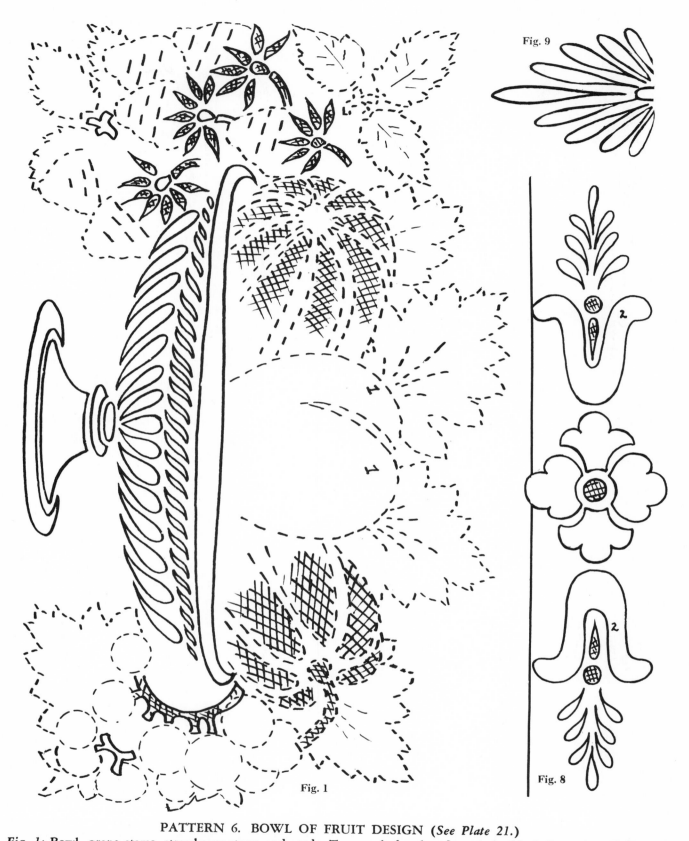

Fig. 9

Fig. 8

Fig. 1

PATTERN 6. BOWL OF FRUIT DESIGN (*See Plate 21.*)

Fig. 1: Bowl, grape stems, strawberry stems and seeds. Trace only bowl and stems in *black lines. Dotted lines* are guides only. Crosshatching is silver. *Fig. 8:* Seat front and top-rail "pillow." Crosshatching is silver. If "pillow" is small, use only rosette and end leaves. Omit tulips marked 2. *Fig. 9:* Top of side-post.

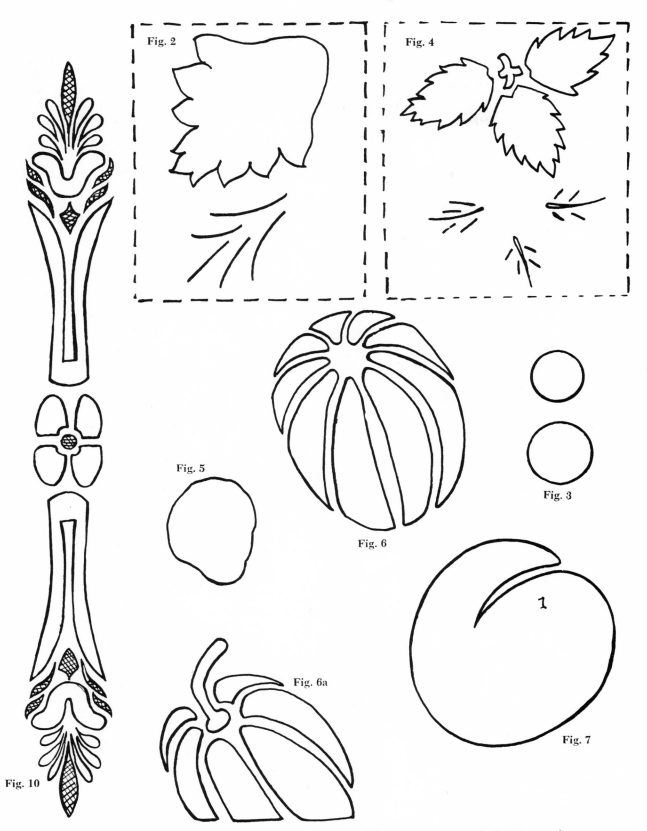

Fig. 2: Grape leaf and vein. Cut on 1 piece of linen. Stencil leaf first; leave center dark. Place vein over center and stencil in silver. *Fig. 3:* Grapes. *Fig. 4:* Strawberry leaves and veining. Stencil leaves first; centers fade off and remain dark. Place veins over centers and stencil in silver. *Fig. 5:* Strawberry. Stencil in cluster, placing over seeded sections in *Fig. 1. Fig. 6:* Melon bottom. *Fig. 6a:* Melon top. Place *Figs. 6* and *6a* in bowl. *Fig. 7:* Peach. Rub high lights at spots marked 1. Lower section fades off. *Fig. 10:* Side-posts. Crosshatching is silver.

PLATE 22. Hitchcock chair. Modern reproduction with copy of authentic old built-up stencil.
*Owned by Mr. and Mrs. Henderson Inches, Jr.,
Chestnut Hill, Mass.*

2. Dip striping brush into paint, and try several practice strokes before working on chair. When brush makes a clean steady line, you are ready to apply stripe to chair.

3. Examine Plate 21 to see where striping should go.

4. Paint the yellow stripe to outline the structure of chair.

5. Do the ball turnings in gold. For this, mix Rich Gold Powder with a little varnish and apply to the turnings with a ¾ inch camels-hair brush. Apply gold on front side of turnings only. Allow to dry.

FINISHING

(Complete chair according to directions. Read Chapter 3 on Final Finishing.)

10

Boston Rockers

NO ONE seems to know exactly where the so-called "Boston rockers" were first made. They may even have come from Connecticut rather than Boston, Massachusetts. Wherever their origin, they became popular, and between 1825 and 1875 were produced in different parts of the country by many craftsmen.

There was good reason for their popularity. They were sturdy, inexpensive, and last but not least, comfortable. Esther Stevens Brazer, who was among the first students of antique furniture to explore the background of these rocking chairs, said that, on examining one of her own family heirlooms, she was amazed to find the rockers on the chair worn completely flat. She had always remembered as a child seeing her grandmother sitting in this chair and the secret of the worn rockers was explained when, in talking with older members of the family, she found that the old lady had rocked every one of her six children to sleep in that chair.

Even the sturdiest of hickory rockers could become flat under such loving wear and tear. The story points out what an important place in family life these rocking chairs played. No home in the late 1800s was complete without a Boston rocker.

Today a drive through New England in the summer will reveal on the porch of almost every farm a Boston rocker painted green, dark brown, or possibly white, with a little red cushion at the top of the back to rest a weary head. These comfortable roll-seated chairs with their capacious backs and sturdy arms invite relaxation, and are every year becoming more popular with amateur antique collectors.

Many people buy and scrape them down to the bare wood, refinishing them in their natural maple or hickory. Charming as these are in rooms furnished with pine or maple, it is more authentic to paint the chairs and to decorate the back-slat with bronze stenciling, or, in the case of some of the

PLATE 24. Head-piece early Boston rocker.
Bowl of Fruit design.
Restored by the author.

late Bostons, with a combination of stenciling and freehand painting. There was variety in the background colors. They were yellow, gray, and dark green, but undoubtedly the bulk of them were black or the well-known imitation-mahogany. In my travels I have seen one in barn-red in Pennsylvania. It is a rather common trait of the Pennsylvania-made chairs to have the arms left in the natural wood (often cherry) and occasionally the seats were left natural, too, or painted a lighter color. In the late chairs, seats were sometimes caned.

In placing the date of a Boston rocker there are many pitfalls, for makers seemed to have taken delight in putting a "late"-type back on an "early"-type base, and vice-versa.

There is a very early type of Boston rocker, as in Pattern 7, which shows clearly the transition from the Windsor chair. This type has a flat, almost round, seat, rather than the bulkier roll-seat. These flat-seated rockers are harder to find than those with the more standard roll-seat fronts, partly because they are older and partly because they were never made in quantity. Boston rockers were produced in every one of the Lambert Hitchcock chair factories from Hitchcocksville to Unionville. There are also files of old newspapers which show advertising for Boston rockers made in Massachusetts, Connecticut, New York, Ohio, Pennsylvania, and Maryland, so it is small wonder that today, a hundred years later, these chairs may still be acquired without too long a search. They may be restored to fresh beauty by your own clever hands to give a comfortable, homelike look to any room.

Head-piece of early Boston rocker—crest-top

Head-piece of early Boston rocker—crest-top

Headpiece for late Boston rocker

Crest-Back Boston Rocker with Gold-Leaf

THE two Boston rockers discussed here are examples of the early type with crested back. The gold-leaf design (see Frontispiece), is the earlier of the two. It shows the rounded Windsor influence in the seat. The signature, "Hitchcock Alford and Co.," which appears on the back, places it *circa* 1832. The Fruit-Cluster design, Plate 24, shows the heavily rolled plank seat, characteristic of later chairs. This chair has a restored design rather than the original decoration.

GOLD-LEAF DESIGN

STEP-BY-STEP DIRECTIONS
PREPARATION

(Refer to Chapter 2, Preparation for Decorating.)

BACKGROUND

Refer to Chapter 3, Painted Finishes. Choose antique black or satin black for most effective background for gold-leaf and stenciling.

APPLYING THE PATTERN

1. Trace Fig. 1, Fig. 3, Fig. 5, and Fig. 6 on heavy transparent tracing paper.
2. Trace Fig. 2, Fig. 2a and Fig. 4 on architects-linen.

CUTTING THE STENCILS

(Refer to Chapter 5, Cutting the Stencil.) Cut Fig. 2, Fig. 2a, and Fig. 4 according to directions. Cut each stencil on a separate piece of linen and leave a margin around each.

TRANSFERRING THE GOLD-LEAF DESIGN

1. Fold tracing of Fig. 1 on dotted line at extreme left and trace in reverse to complete central unit of design.
2. Fold Fig. 5 on dotted line at left, and trace.
3. Fold this tracing in center, and trace whole thing in reverse, thus completing motif for front of chair. (See Frontispiece.)
4. Find center of top-slat with tape measure and place Fig. 1 in position (see Frontispiece), leaving enough room at top and bottom of slat to add stenciled border, Fig. 7.
5. Cover back of tracing with white chalk.
6. Place pattern chalk-side down on slat, and draw over pattern with medium-hard pencil. Lift tracing. The pattern should remain on chair in white outline.
7. Make a second tracing of Fig. 3, in reverse, so that curved acanthus leaf will fit left side of slat.
8. Number this tracing Fig. 3a.
9. Cover both Fig. 3 and Fig. 3a with white chalk or lithopone-powder.
10. Place Fig. 3 on right end of slat, fitting curve to curve of chair. Transfer by drawing over design with pencil.
11. Repeat at right end of slat, using tracing Fig. 3a.
12. Transfer tracing Fig. 5 to front of seat in same manner.

APPLYING THE GOLD-LEAF

(Refer to Chapter 6, Gold-Leaf, and read entire section.)

1. Paint gold-leaf undercoat on designs which

have been transferred to chair, taking care to keep the paint coat thin and even, with sharp outlines.

2. Let surface get tacky. Test with tip of finger to determine "right tack."

3. Apply gold-leaf according to directions.

4. Allow chair to dry for 3 or 4 days before attempting to stencil remainder of pattern.

SHADING THE GOLD-LEAF

1. Apply veining as shown in Fig. 1 and Fig. 3 with a crow-quill pen and black drawing-ink. Follow diagram carefully for position. Be sure all rough edges have been cleaned off and touched up on gold-leaf design before varnishing.

APPLYING THE STENCILS

1. Varnish entire top-slat including gold-leaf. Allow to dry 24 hours.

2. Apply thin coat of varnish to area where stenciling appears in design. (Fig. 2, Fig. 2a, Fig. 3, and Fig. 4.)

3. When tacky, apply stencils. Sections showing cross-hatching are stenciled in Aluminum Powder, remainder in Pale Gold.

4. Allow to dry, and wipe off excess bronze powder with a damp cloth.

SIDE-POSTS AND FRONT LEGS

1. Paint a brush-stroke design in coach yellow on side-posts and front legs of rocker. (Refer to Chapter 4 for recipe for authentic striping yellow and instructions in brush-stroke painting.)

2. Transfer design to chair from tracing and paint pattern using a No. 12 pointed sable brush. Allow to dry.

STRIPING

1. Refer to Chapter 4, section on Striping, and follow directions.

2. Examine Frontispiece for placing of striping on top-slat, side-posts, and seat. Color should be authentic striping yellow.

FINISHING

(Refer to Chapter 3, Final Finishing.) Complete chair according to directions.

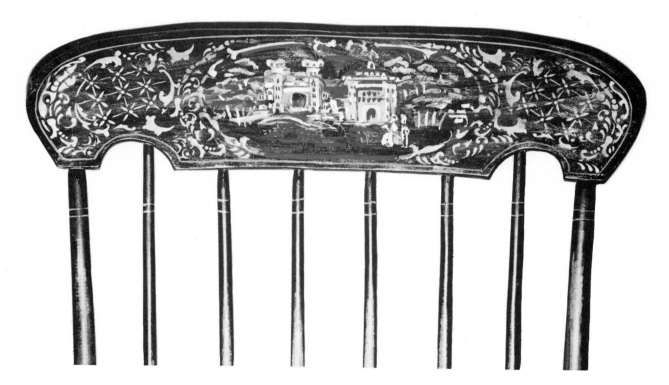

PLATE 25. Head-piece late Boston rocker, after 1850.
Owned and restored by the author.

PATTERN 7. GOLD-LEAF DESIGN. (*See Frontispiece.*)

Fig. 1: Central motif; in gold-leaf. *Fig. 2:* Rosette; in Rich Gold and Aluminum. *Fig. 2a:* Continuation of rosette motif; in Aluminum. *Fig. 3:* Acanthus leaf; in gold-leaf. *Fig. 4:* Small rosette; in Aluminum. *Fig. 5:* Motif for front of seat; in gold-leaf. *Fig. 6:* Leaf motif; in brush-stroke painting. *Fig. 7:* Running border for top and bottom.

PLATE 26. Early crest-back Boston rocker. Fruit Cluster design. See Pattern 8.
Owned by Miss Katharine Garrett, Pliny Farm, Lyman, New Hampshire.

Crest-Back Boston Rocker with Fruit-Cluster Design

STEP-BY-STEP DIRECTIONS

PREPARATION

Refer to Chapter 2, Preparing Chairs for Decoration.

BACKGROUND

Refer to Chapter 3, Painted Finishes.

Antique black, satin-black, or imitation-rosewood are appropriate background colors.

APPLYING THE DECORATION

Tracing the pattern

Trace on separate pieces of architects-linen Fig. 1, Fig. 2, Fig. 3, Fig. 4, Fig. 5, Fig. 6, Fig. 7, Fig. 9, and Fig. 10. Trace Figs. 8 and 8a on one piece of linen. (Fig. 11 should not be traced as it is to be used only as a reference diagram in placing units of the pattern.)

Cutting the stencils

Refer to Chapter 5, Cutting the Stencil, and follow directions. Cut each stencil on a separate piece of linen except Fig. 8 and Fig. 8a, which should be kept together. Leave margin around each stencil.

Applying the stencil

Refer to Chapter 5, Varnishing before Stenciling and Applying the Stencil. When varnish is tacky, you are ready to stencil.

1. Place *peach*, Fig. 1, in center of top slat, as in reference diagram, Fig. 11. Stencil in Pale Gold, carefully shading high lights as marked with diagonal lines, and allowing gold to fade off to form shadows. (Refer to Chapter 5.)

2. Apply *pineapple*, Fig. 2, in **Rich Gold** or **Bronze.** Allow pineapple to fade off behind peach.

3. Apply *pear*, Fig. 3, in same manner, to right of peach.

4. Apply *flower*, Fig. 4, in two positions beneath peach, and in two positions at top of cluster. See Fig. 11.

5. Apply *flower petals*, Fig. 5, and *flower bud*, Fig. 6, as indicated in Fig. 11, using Aluminum Powder for sections which show crosshatching, and Rich Gold for the remainder.

6. Apply *grapes*, Fig. 7, in Aluminum, as indicated in Fig. 11.

7. Apply *leaf*, Fig. 8, and *veining*, Fig. 8a, in several different background positions as indicated in Fig. 11. Stencil leaf inward from tips, allowing center to fade into shadow. Stencil veining in Aluminum over shadowy center.

8. Apply *scroll*, Fig. 7, in Rich Gold at each end of top-slat, adjusting stencil to curve of slat and leaving room for a narrow yellow stripe of coach-yellow around edge of slat.

9. After applying scroll at one end, clean off excess gold powder with carbon tetrachloride, and stencil in reverse position at other end.

10. Apply Fig. 10 on rolled section at front of seat. See Plate 24. Center of seat may be located exactly by measuring front seat-rail with tape measure, taking care not to damage tacky varnish. Fig. 10 is one-half of motif. Stencil one-half, clean off excess gold, and reverse stencil to complete motif.

11. When all stenciling is thoroughly dry, wipe off with damp cloth to remove loose gold powder.

Fig. 6

Fig. 7

Fig. 9

Top

Fig. 1

Fig. 2

Fig. 3

Fig. 5

Fig. 4

PATTERN 8. FRUIT CLUSTER DESIGN (*See Plate 26*)

Fig. 1: Peach. *Fig. 2:* Pineapple. *Fig. 3:* Pear. *Fig. 4:* Flower. *Fig. 5:* Flower bud. *Fig. 6:* Flower bud. *Fig. 7:* Bunch of grapes and stem. *Fig. 9:* Scroll.

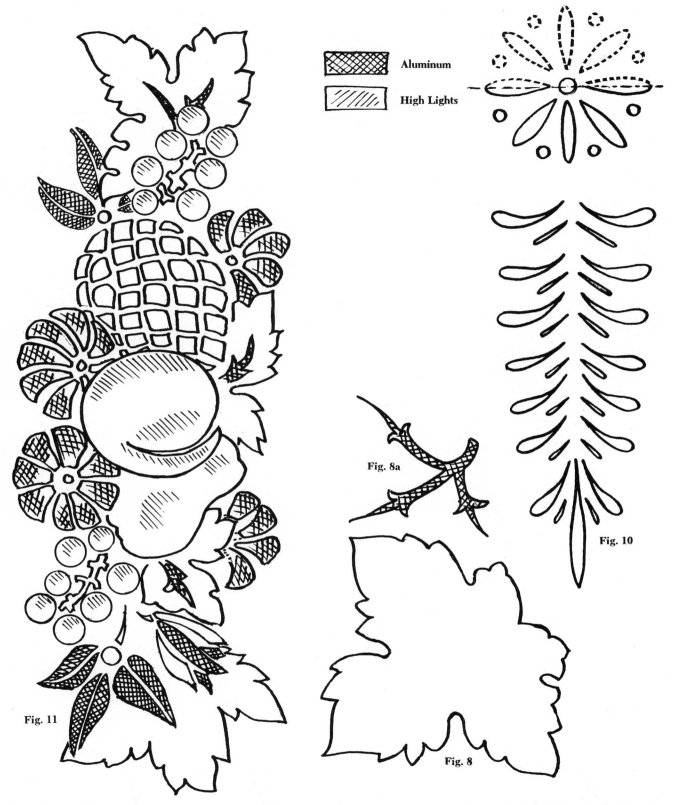

Aluminum

High Lights

Fig. 11

Fig. 8a

Fig. 10

Fig. 8

Fig. 8: Grape leaf. *Fig. 8a:* Veining. *Fig. 10:* Half of motif for front seat. Reverse to complete design. *Fig. 11:* Reference diagram of complete fruit cluster design.

Refer to Chapter 4, section on Striping, and use authentic coach-yellow to apply stripes. Plate 24 will indicate placing of stripes.

Read Chapter 3, Final Finishing, and complete chair according to directions.

PLATE 27. Late Boston rocker. Stenciled design with painted medallion. See Pattern 9.
Owned and restored by the author.

A Late-Type Boston Rocker

THE Boston rocker, Plate 27, is the most common type, still found in antique shops or friendly attics. The rolled plank-seat and simple rounded top-slat are typical of the rockers which were turned out in great quantity by many chairmakers from 1860 on. These chairs are sturdy and comfortable and may be painted to fit in with almost any decorative scheme. It should be mentioned that the original Boston rockers were almost always painted rather than finished in the natural wood, and to restore them with any degree of authenticity they should be painted rather than scraped down. This chair is decorated with a design which combines bronze stenciling and freehand painting.

STEP-BY-STEP DIRECTIONS

MATERIALS

1. *For background*

   Flat black or enamel-undercoat in color of your choice

   Avoid enamels as the high gloss is not a good background for decorating

   ½ pint spar-varnish

   ½ pint satin-varnish

   ½ pint turpentine

   2 medium-sized paintbrushes, one for paint, one for varnish

2. *For applying design*

   Bronze powders, in Rich Gold and Pale Gold

   Architects-linen for stencil, about 12 inches square

   Artists-oil tube-paints in permanent green, chrome green, yellow ochre, chrome-yellow medium, alizarin crimson, cadmium red, burnt sienna, lamp-black, Titanium White, cobalt blue, mauve

   No. 3 pointed water-color brush

   No. 12 artist's sable or camels-hair brush

   Quill striping brush with 2-inch hairs for narrow striping

BACKGROUND

Refer to Chapter 2, section on Preparing Chairs for Decorating, and Chapter 3, Background Finishes. If an old design is visible on your chair, see also Chapter 1, section on Preserving Old Designs. After chair has been painted in the color of your choice, it is ready for decorating.

CUTTING THE STENCILS

1. Place architects-linen, glossy side down, over scroll pattern Fig. 2, and trace with medium-hard pencil. Do not trace dotted lines.

2. Make tracing of Fig. 3. Leave an inch wide margin on all four sides when you cut stencils.

3. Refer to Chapter 5, Cutting the Stencil, and cut out Fig. 2 and Fig. 3.

TRANSFERRING THE FLOWER MOTIF

1. Trace outlines of Fig. 4 on good quality tracing paper, making no attempt to trace shading.

2. Place this tracing of Fig. 4 on dotted lines of Fig. 2, matching up "line and circle" border to complete an oval frame around flowers.

3. Trace dotted section of Fig. 2 in solid lines.

4. Do the flower motif and surrounding "line and circle" border freehand rather than with a stencil.

5. To transfer the pattern from tracing paper to chair back, rub back of tracing with lithopone-powder or with black charcoal, depending on whether you are transferring to a light or dark background. Place tracing, powder side down, on

top-slat, and fasten it into position with masking tape. With a medium-hard pencil, draw over the design. When tracing paper is removed, an outline of pattern should show clearly on the chair.

PAINTING THE FLOWER MOTIF

The painted motif contains a white rose, a red rose with buds, red strawberries, white blossoms, green leaves, and scrolls. Use a No. 12 pointed water-color brush for large units of pattern, a No. 3 fine-pointed scroll brush for smaller leaves, petals, and scrolls. Mix a painting base of 1 tablespoon of varnish diluted with 1 teaspoon of turpentine. A large jar cap makes a good container for this.

1. Mix on a palette permanent green with a little black and a little white, and add just enough of the varnish to allow it to flow easily. Add more white if color is so dark it will not show up against your background.

2. Paint all the *leaves* with this green.

3. Before they have dried, mix chrome green with white and a dash of yellow, diluting with the varnish, and paint a high light on each leaf beginning at the tip and letting the light color blend into the dark. On the large leaf beneath the roses, the light shading comes on the lower half of the leaf. Use a little pure yellow to give the effect of sunlight in this delicate shading. After painting in the main areas of light and dark green, allow the leaves to dry. Dots and cross-hatching indicate light and shadow.

4. With the fine-pointed brush, paint fine *veining* and *stems* in the lighter green.

5. Clean brush with turpentine and block in white *strawberry blossoms.*

6. Before these have dried, shade a little yellow from the tip toward the center of each petal. Now with a bit of mauve on the tip of your brush, lightly suggest a little purple shadow near the center of the petals, marked with dots.

7. Paint *centers* in chrome yellow.

8. Mix alizarin crimson and cadmium red with a bit of white and paint *strawberries,* ignoring shading. Mix a darker tone by adding burnt umber to alizarin and work shading with an almost dry brush,

following cross-hatching in Fig. 4. Allow to dry. Do not paint seed markings at this time.

9. For *red rose* and *buds* marked 1, mix light pink by adding small amounts of alizarin crimson and cadmium red to white. Paint rose and buds, ignoring shading. Allow to dry, then over-paint rose and buds with clear varnish. Allow varnish to dry to tacky stage. Using an almost dry brush, work a deeper shade of pink into dotted area. Mix a still deeper red tone by combining alizarin and cadmium with burnt umber. Work in shadows indicated by cross-hatching. The damp varnish will float shadow color into the lighter sections. Allow rose to dry before outlining petals with very light pink. (Section 11c.)

10. For *white rose* marked 2, mix white with a speck of mauve and yellow and paint entire flower. When dry, over-paint with clear varnish. Let varnish dry until tacky. For shadows, add a speck of burnt umber to mauve. Work color into damp varnish with an almost dry brush. Follow shading lines in pattern and let varnish float color into lighter sections of rose. Allow to dry before outlining petals. (Section 11a.)

11. After twenty-four hours add the finishing touches to this design.

a. With pure white mixed in a little varnish, suggest the structure of the *white rose* by outlining petals. Follow chart of Fig. 4 for degrees of shading, keeping white sections very light, and allowing dotted and lined sections to fade into each other gradually.

b. Outline tips of petals sharply with the white paint to give depth to the center of flower.

c. For the *red rose* use light pink to show the high lights and to outline the petals. Follow the drawing of the roses in Fig. 4 to model the petals.

d. Add seeds to the strawberries by taking the yellow you used for the centers of the strawberry blossoms and following the seed lines in Fig. 4.

e. Mix yellow ochre with a little white and chrome-yellow medium and shade the veining in the leaves. Use a very fine brush for this and keep the brush almost dry.

f. After this veining has dried, add thin shadows on the darker portion of the leaves with a thin transparent wash of alizarin red. Mix just a touch of alizarin with clear varnish and brush in the shadow.

STENCILING THE SCROLLS

1. Varnish the entire top-slat and allow to dry until tacky.

2. Place the stencil of Fig. 2 at the left of the flower motif. The outside edge of the scroll when stenciled should be ¾ of an inch in from the edge.

3. Rub on Rich Gold Powder with no shading.

4. Wipe off stencil with cleaning fluid, reverse it, and stencil the scroll on the right. Allow to dry, then wipe off excess powder with a damp cloth.

STRIPING

(Refer to Chapter 4, section on Striping.) Make a narrow stripe around the outside edge of the curved top slat. The line should be about ¼ inch inside the edge. Hold brush steady by guiding with the little finger.

DECORATING THE CHAIR SEAT

Fig. 5 shows placement of stencil and striping on seat. Fig. 5a is an alternate treatment of seat.

1. Give entire seat a coat of spar-varnish.

2. When varnish has dried to tacky stage, apply Fig. 3, stenciling in Rich Gold. This motify is especially appropriate for the roll-front type of seat.

3. Allow varnish to dry for 24 hours. When dry, wipe excess gold powder from stencil with a damp cloth.

4. With white chalk or a black charcoal stick, depending on whether you are working on a light or dark background, block in striping lines, using Fig. 5 or Fig. 5a as a guide. Striping on seat should be in same color as that on top slat. For the wider stripe, it may be easier to paint two fine lines, ⅛ of an inch apart, and fill in space between lines with a pointed water-color brush, than to attempt to make the wide line with a striping quill. The final effect is almost the same, so employ the method that seems easier to you.

FINISHING

Refer to Chapter 3, section Final Finishing, and follow directions to complete decoration of chair.

Alternate pattern for use in central medallion of late Boston rocker

Fig. 4

Fig. 2

PATTERN 9. LATE-TYPE BOSTON ROCKER (*See Plate 27.*)

Fig. 2: Stenciled scroll at left side of top-slat. For right side, reverse the stencil. *Fig. 4:* Brush-stroke painting pattern for center of top-slat.

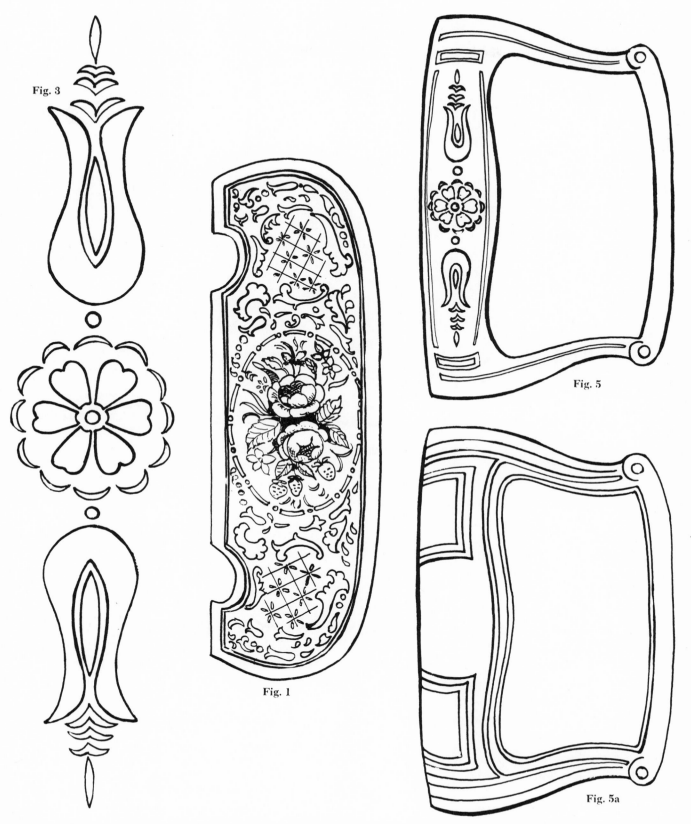

Fig. 1: Reference drawing of back-slat showing placement of design elements. *Fig. 3:* Stenciled motif on front of seat. *Fig. 5:* Reference drawing for front of seat. *Fig. 5a:* Alternate treatment for front of seat.

11
Nineteenth-Century Fiddle Backs

Design for fiddle-back chair by William Eaton

A POPULAR chair in the latter half of the nineteenth century was the fiddle-back, sometimes inaccurately called "banister-back" because the back slat was cut to resemble the large turned newel post on a staircase. This chair had either a simple flat top-rail about four inches wide and curved at the top, or the more elaborate "crest-top". The crest-top chairs were usually made in finer woods and the back-slat was more intricately cut. For decoration, the maker often relied on the simulated-grain finish alone, with a neat yellow striping to point up the structure of the chair. This graining and imitation of expensive burled woods was so skillfully done by early artisans that the chair needed no other decoration. There were, however, many such chairs which had elaborate bronze stenciling for decoration. After 1875, designs were made that combined colorful hand-painted flower sprays with gold scrolls and stenciling.

William Eaton, the artful stencil-cutter who worked for many years in New Boston, New Hampshire, left many cut-outs for fiddle-back chairs. Some of Eaton's stencils are most intricate and are among the finest examples of clever cut-work we have. Although they are marvels as show pieces of the stencil-cutter's art, the designs themselves are somewhat sentimental and elaborate. Once again it should be pointed out that the finest designs in stenciling are those first, strong, built-up or many-unit stencils of the early nineteenth century.

Stenciled Fiddle-Back Chair

THIS old fiddle-back chair was in poor condition and it seemed wise to remove finish and decoration and restore it from the bare wood. Chairs of this type are not rare; they may be picked up at auctions or antique shops, and they are comparatively inexpensive. With an elaborate stenciled decoration such as this, they make interesting desk or side chairs. They also look well in pairs in front halls or vestibules. (Plate 28).

STEP-BY-STEP DIRECTIONS

MATERIALS

½ pint flat-black

½ pint Venetian or barn-red (if rosewood finish is desired)

½ pint spar-varnish

½ pint satin-varnish

2 medium-sized paintbrushes, one for varnishing, one for painting

Stencil powders: Rich Gold, Pale Gold, Aluminum

Architects-linen

Frosted acetate

Small piece chamois or velvet for stenciling

Quill striping brush

Artists-oils: yellow ochre, chrome-yellow medium, burnt umber

BACKGROUND

Refer to Chapter 2, section on Preparing Chairs for Decorating, and Chapter 3, section on Satin-Black Finish or Imitation-Rosewood Finish.

1. Prepare chair in color of your choice.

2. Rub smooth with 6/0 sandpaper or fine steel wool.

CUTTING THE STENCIL

1. Select a piece of architects-linen an inch

larger on all four sides than Fig. 2. This pattern is the left half of top-slat of chair, and you will cut only this much of the pattern for the stencil. Reverse this stencil to make the right half and also complete the top-slat design.

2. Place linen, glossy side down, on Fig. 2, and with a medium-hard pencil trace the pattern. Include outer lines as these will serve as a guide for striping.

3. Refer to Chapter 5, section on Cutting the

PLATE 28.

Nineteenth century Fiddle-back chair. See Pattern 10.
Owned and restored by the author.

Stencil, and cut out the design.

4. Trace also Fig. 4 and Fig. 5, making entire tracing of both parts on same piece of architects-linen, and fitting pattern together as you trace. Completed tracing should look like Fig. 3. (Do not trace Fig. 3. It is a reference sketch.)

5. Trace Fig. 6, the side-post decoration.

6. Trace Fig. 7, the motif for seat-rail.

7. Cut all stencils and number them.

APPLYING THE STENCILS

1. Place chair in horizontal position on low table with top-slat facing you.

2. Apply thin coat spar-varnish to central back-slat or "fiddle". Allow to dry to tacky stage.

3. Refer to Chapter 5, section Directions for Stenciling.

4. Place stencil which contains Fig. 4 and Fig. 5 on the slat, making certain that it is centered and in a straight position.

5. Refer to Fig. 3. Rub Aluminum Powder into the parts of the pattern in Fig. 3 which are cross-hatched.

6. Rub Rich Gold and Pale Gold at random in the remaining holes of the stencil.

7. Carefully remove stencil from the tacky varnish so excess gold dust does not spill.

8. Give top-slat and side-posts of chair a coat of varnish. Allow to dry to tacky stage.

9. Apply Fig. 6, the leaf pattern, to side-posts, using Aluminum for grapes and tendrils, and Pale Gold for leaves.

10. Remove stencil.

11. Locate center of top-slat. Place Fig. 2 in position to apply half the top-slat pattern.

12. Rub in Rich Gold and Aluminum-Powder, referring to Fig. 1 as a color guide. The parts of Fig. 1 which show cross-hatching should be done in silver, the remainder in gold.

13. Remove stencil and scrub stencil-linen clean with a damp cloth dipped in carbon tetrachloride.

14. Reverse the stencil and apply other half of design.

15. Varnish front of seat.

16. When it has dried to tacky stage, apply Fig. 7 in the center.

17. Allow chair to dry for at least 24 hours; then sponge off with a damp cloth to remove excess gold powder.

18. When dry, give entire chair a coat of varnish.

STRIPING

Refer to Chapter 4, section on Striping. Read instructions carefully and practice with striping quill. Follow the pattern for striping in photograph of the chair, Plate 28.

FINISHING

Refer to Chapter 3, section on Final Finishing, and follow directions to complete decoration of chair.

Note: The elaborate stencils for this chair may be used separately for other furniture. The running-leaf pattern on the side-posts, in particular, makes an attractive border for small tables or chests. The top-slat may be adapted as a decoration for a bureau, commode or dresser.

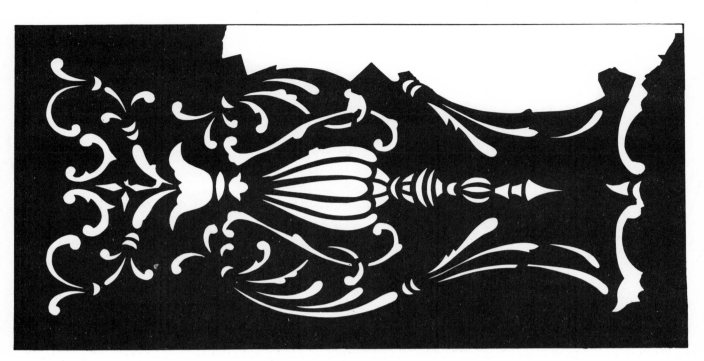

PLATE 29. Stencil for chair-back. Cutting and Morrow Collection.
Courtesy Metropolitan Museum of Art, New York City.

PLATE 30. Stencil for cross-piece. Cutting and Morrow Collection.
Courtesy Metropolitan Museum of Art, New York City.

PLATE 31. Stencil for top-slat. Cutting and Morrow Collection.
Courtesy Metropolitan Museum of Art, New York City.

PATTERN 10. STENCILED FIDDLE-BACK (*See Plate 2.*)

Fig. 1: Entire top-slat pattern in miniature. *Fig. 2:* Full-size pattern for one-half of top-slat. *Fig. 7:* Motif for front seat-rail.

Fig. 3: Sketch of middle back-slat in miniature. *Fig. 4:* Upper half of back-slat. *Fig. 5:* Lower half of back-slat. *Figs.* 4 and 5 should be interlocked in tracing, as parts of a jig-saw puzzle. *Fig. 6:* Pattern for side-posts.

[107]

12

Anybody's Chair—Unclassified Type

THERE is another category of chairs to be found in almost anybody's attic or barn. These chairs are old, fifty or seventy-five years perhaps, but not quite old enough to fall into the group of named antiques. At the turn of the century, they appeared as side chairs in bedroom sets. Sometimes we find them in black walnut as dining chairs in a Victorian dining room set, and I have seen them by the dozen in quaint village churches throughout New England where they were used as extra seats in church or as social chairs in the parish house. Most of them had caned seats and two back-slats, and they lend themselves quite charmingly to the amateur-painter's brush.

We have included three patterns which may be used to decorate these chairs. They may be adapted to almost any width slat and, by wise selection of the background color, you may bring "anybody's chair" into the color scheme and period of the room you are redecorating.

You may choose a light or dark base color for your chair, but if you use the Classic Leaf for gold stenciling, it will be more effective on a black or very dark background.

The Moss Rose pattern and the Camellia pattern are equally attractive on a light-colored chair. Sea green, French blue, yellow, or Chinese vermilion are effective background colors for these chairs, and when completed they may be used for a bright accent in a sun-room, bedroom, or breakfast room.

Do not be satisfied with just painting a chair and applying a decal or transfer in the middle of the back-slat. Your chair will lack unity and style unless you plan its decoration as a whole, with some form of striping to point up architectural lines and turnings.

We do not include working directions for these three chairs but will discuss use of the patterns in a general way. You will find specific instructions in Chapters 1, 3, 4, and 5, which will make it easy for you to adapt the patterns to your own needs. It should be fun to paint this particular "ungraded" chair for it is not so necessary to hold to an authentic type of decoration as it is in restoring a good Hitchcock or Sheraton fancy chair. "Anybody's chair" was not very rare to begin with, so you may give free rein to your decorative fancy. Perhaps under your clever fingers it will gain the personality it never had before.

PLATE 32. Anybody's chair. To be decorated with Patterns 11, 12, or 13.

Moss Rose Design

THIS famous old pattern is done entirely with oil paints and a brush, in the so-called brush-stroke technique. It is appropriate for a chair of almost any color and is especially effective with a pastel background of ivory, aqua-green, or French gray. Plate 32 shows a chair for which this design would be suitable.

Moss rose design for anybody's chair

STEP-BY-STEP DIRECTIONS
TRANSFERRING THE DESIGN

1. Refer to Chapter 6, section on Tracing and Transferring the Design, and follow directions.

2. Transfer a line drawing of Pattern 11, disregarding diagonal shading and dots on pattern, as these lines are only for a guide in painting the design. Pattern is equal to one-half of design.

PAINTING THE PATTERN

1. Assemble these colors (artists-oils): alizarin crimson, cadmium red, yellow ochre, chrome-yellow medium, chrome green, permanent green, mauve, ultramarine blue, black, and white.

2. Combine 2 tablespoons of spar-varnish with 1 tablespoon of turpentine in a small container. This mixture is the painting medium or size.

3. Mix 6 small batches of paint, using the varnish and turpentine mixture to moisten the paint.

a. *Light pink:* alizarin, white, with a speck of yellow.

b. *Rose:* alizarin, cadmium red, burnt sienna, with small amounts of white and blue (very little blue, please!).

c. *Dark rose:* alizarin, burnt sienna, blue, keeping alizarin the dominant color.

d. *Light green:* chrome green, white with a

small amount of chrome yellow medium.

e. *Dark green:* permanent green, with small amounts of yellow, black and alizarin.

f. *Off-white:* white, with small amounts of yellow and mauve.

4. Paint the entire *rose* and all *buds* in light pink. With the buds be careful to paint only the petal sections pink. The surrounding leaf and thorn portions are, of course, green.

5. Shade the *rose* before the paint dries. To shade the rose, refer to pattern, and paint dotted section of petals in rose color. Keep brush rather dry and work rose color into the light pink so colors merge a little. Dip brush into dark rose and paint the deepest shadow in this color, allowing it to fade

[109]

into the rose tone. Allow to dry.

6. Paint all *leaves, tendrils, stems,* and *cup parts of buds* in light green.

7. Shade the *leaves* by painting portions with dark green, working the dark color into the light where they merge, with an almost-dry brush. Outline underside of *stems* with a fine line of dark green. Outline shadow on *bud cups* in dark green. Allow to dry.

8. When painting has dried, high-light *roses and leaves* with off-white, keeping the brush only partly filled with paint to make a controlled line. To high-light leaves, use an almost-dry brush. Dip it in the off-white paint and indicate *veining* as in pattern.

STRIPING

1. Refer to Chapter 4, section on Striping. Examine the diagrams for striping chair-seats and backs, and select the one most suitable for your chair.

2. Draw guide-lines lightly with chalk in places on chair where you wish striping to appear.

3. Paint stripes in color of your choice, following directions in Chapter 4. The following color suggestions may help you in choosing:

a. *For light backgrounds:* bluish green stripe in ⅜-inch width used in conjunction with a 1/16-inch stripe in black or coach yellow.

b. *For dark backgrounds:* authentic striping yellow is recommended. Off-white striping is also proper if you prefer it. See Chapter 4, section on Colors for Striping.

FINISHING

1. Refer to Chapter 3, section Final Finishing, and follow the step-by-step directions.

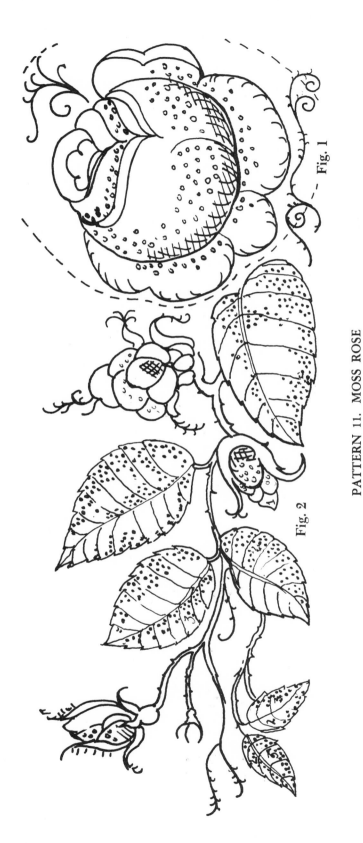

Fig. 1

Fig. 2

PATTERN 11. MOSS ROSE

Fig. 1: Central motif. *Fig. 2:* Left side motif. For right side, reverse tracing to complete pattern. Dots on flower indicate *medium rose*, dots on leaves indicate *medium green*, and cross-hatching indicates darkest tone in each case.

Classic-Leaf Design

THE CLASSIC LEAF, a stencil pattern, is striking on a black, dark green, or dark red chair. The bronze-powder stenciling is not so effective when used on pastel backgrounds. Plate 32 shows a chair for which this design is suitable. Because of its extreme simplicity, however, the Classic Leaf is readily adapted to almost any chair with a top-slat four inches or so wide. We have also stenciled this design on other furniture. A small black bedside table was handsomely decorated with the Classic Leaf carried out in gold and silver as the main motif for the drawer front. The only other decoration on the table was a fine striping line in coach yellow framing the stenciling on the drawer and outlining the table-top. Following are directions for placing this design on a two-slat chair similar to picture.

STEP-BY-STEP DIRECTIONS
CUTTING THE STENCIL

1. Refer to Chapter 5 and read entire section, Notes on Stenciling Techniques. Follow step-by-step directions in cutting the stencils.

2. Trace Pattern 12 on two separate pieces of architects-linen. One section is the central motif, Fig. 1 at right of dotted line; the other is the side section at left of dotted line, Fig. 2.

3. Cut the stencil.

APPLYING THE STENCIL

1. Apply a thin coat of varnish to top-slat and middle-slat of chair and allow to dry until tacky. Chair should be in horizontal position on a low work table.

2. Place central motif in center of middle-slat and stencil it. The cross-hatching indicates portion to be stenciled in Aluminum; the remainder is in two shades of gold powder, perhaps Rich Gold and Brushed Brass.

3. Place central motif in center of top-slat and stencil it.

4. Place side section in position at left of central motif and stencil it.

5. After cleaning stencil with carbon tetrachloride, reverse stencil of side section and stencil it at right of central motif to complete design on top-slat. Allow to dry.

6. For middle-slat, stencil the central motif only.

STRIPING

1. Refer to Chapter 4, section on Striping. Examine the diagrams and select a striping pattern that seems suitable for your chair.

2. Mark with chalk, directly on chair, light guide lines where striping should appear.

3. Apply striping in either gold or authentic striping yellow. See Chapter 4, section on Striping.

FINISHING

1. Refer to Chapter 3, section on Final Finishing, and follow Step-by-Step Directions.

PATTERN 12. CLASSIC LEAF Fig. 1

Fig. 1: Central motif. *Fig. 2:* Left side motif. For right side, reverse stencil to complete pattern.

Fig. 2

Fig. 1

Classic leaf stencil for anybody's chair

Camellia Design (Oil-Stencil Technique)

THE Camellia design, Pattern 13, is not old, but a design created in response to requests for a naturalistic flower-design that could be applied with a stencil. The inspiration for my drawings came from the beautiful Camellia Gardens in Norfolk, Virginia, where I made sketches from the flowers as they were actually growing. The exquisitely-fashioned flower lends itself well to decorative design, and we hope that as you transfer it to a chair it will bring you a breath of spring in Virginia.

On a dark background, the design may be worked out in several shades of gold and silver powder, using your own creative ability to plan exact gradations of color. Step-by-step instructions

Camellia design

for preparing the background and cutting and applying stencils will be found in Chapters 1, 3, and 5. A chair similar in shape to the one in the picture would be attractive with this pattern as decoration.

The Camellia Pattern is also effective when rendered in a slightly different type of stenciling, a technique that calls for the use of artists-oils and a stiff-bristled brush, instead of gold powders, varnish, and a velvet finger. When applied by this method, the pattern is one of the most versatile in the book, because it may be developed in a variety of color schemes.

STEP-BY-STEP DIRECTIONS

Special materials needed
    Sheet of heavy oiled stencil paper
    Stiff-bristled stencil brush
    Stencil knife
    ½ pint turpentine
    ½ pint spar-varnish
    Artists-oil paints: alizarin crimson, cadmium red, chrome-yellow medium, yellow ochre, permanent green, ultramarine blue, mauve, black, and white

TRANSFERRING THE PATTERN

1. Trace Pattern 13 in two parts: the central unit (at right of dotted line), and the side section (at left). Use transparent tracing paper.

2. Transfer tracing to yellow oiled stencil-cardboard. (See Chapter 6, Tracing and Transferring the Design.) Do not trace dotted lines or shading.

CUTTING THE STENCIL

1. Place stencil-cardboard on a piece of glass

or flat tin.

2. With an Xacto tool or a sharp pocket-knife, cut out each section of the design, being careful not to cut through the bridge sections.

3. If you do slice a bridge by mistake, mend the break by pasting cellophane tape on both sides of the stencil-board and recut the segment through the double tape. If it is difficult for you to cut with the Xacto tool or jack-knife, you may pierce a hole in each segment with sharp-pointed scissors and cut exactly as you would a linen stencil.

COLORS

Mix 5 small batches of paint, using spar-varnish as your medium. Paint mixture should be thick.

1. *Light rose:* Add small amounts of alizarin, cadmium red, and yellow ochre to white, using a very little varnish to moisten. Keep color very light.

2. *Dark rose:* Mix alizarin, cadmium red, burnt sienna, and a small amount of blue with varnish.

3. *Yellow:* Mix chrome yellow medium, yellow ochre, and white with varnish.

Light green: Mix chrome green, white, and small amount of yellow with varnish.

5. *Dark green:* Mix permanent green, white and small amount of black with varnish. This color should be considerably darker in tone than the light green.

STENCILING THE PATTERN

1. Place central unit stencil in position on top-slat of chair and anchor it with thumbtacks.

2. Dip brush in paint mixture and, holding brush in a vertical position, tap paint over open sections of stencil. It is important that the bristles of the brush meet the open holes of the stencil in a vertical position.

3. Stencil *stamens of flowers* in yellow.

4. Stencil *centers of flowers* around stamens in dark rose.

5. Stencil *petals* in light rose.

6. Remove center stencil.

7. Place stencil of side section in position and anchor with thumbtacks.

8. Stencil *tip of each leaf* in light green and *complete leaves* in dark green. Allow the two greens to blend into each other.

9. Stencil *buds* in light rose and dark rose.

10. Stencil *stems* in dark green.

11. Stencil small *scrolls* in light green, and allow paint to dry thoroughly.

12. If colors seem too bright after you have finished stenciling, dim them with a glaze made of burnt sienna mixed with a little burnt umber in turpentine. This glaze should be transparent, not opaque.

13. Moisten a cloth with a few drops of varnish and dip into the paint mixture. Hold stencil in position and tap this color over the entire design with the cloth. If the color seems too dark and obscures the design, wipe excess color with a clean rag until you have dimmed the vivid hues a little, but not too much. Allow to dry.

STRIPING

1. Refer to Chapter 4, section on Striping. Examine the diagrams and select a striping pattern appropriate to your chair.

2. Mark guide lines with chalk directly on chair where striping should appear.

3. Apply striping in color of your choice.

FINISHING

Refer to Chapter 3, section on Final Finishing, and follow step-by-step directions.

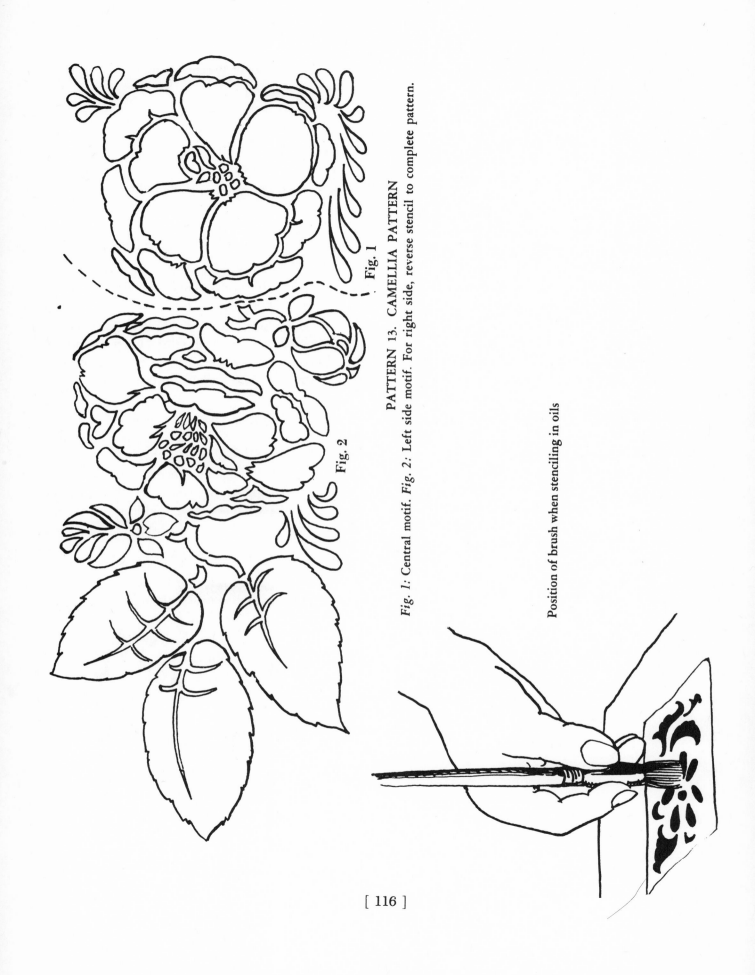

Fig. 1

Fig. 2

PATTERN 13. CAMELLIA PATTERN

Fig. 1: Central motif. *Fig. 2*: Left side motif. For right side, reverse stencil to complete pattern.

Position of brush when stenciling in oils

13

Cohasset Colonial

REPRODUCTIONS of antique ladder-back chairs may be bought knocked-down, and assembled at home. The Cohasset Colonial chair is so called because the maker of this and other knocked-down furniture has named his wares for the town of Cohasset, Massachusetts, home of his shop. The wood is excellent-quality birch, and it is well-sanded and smooth. All the materials and instructions for weaving the seat are included. When the chair is completed, you have a strong and substantial piece of furniture that will last for years.

This chair takes a natural-wood finish very well. It may also be home-finished to simulate walnut or mahogany by rubbing into the raw wood one of the penetrating oil stains. Never use a "varnish stain." Color wood with an oil stain or with artists-oils thinned with turpentine. If you choose to paint the chair and decorate it with a stenciled or painted design, it may be made to fit any color scheme. Possible colors for background are black, dark blue, dark green, barn-red, yellow, or white.

It should be mentioned here that this type of ladder-back chair was not decorated with stencils in colonial days. I have never seen an authentic old ladder-back with a stenciled design. To put any design on this chair, therefore, is somewhat of a departure from the "purist" theory of never using a pattern that is not authentic for the period. However, the ladder-back chair has been developed in many different countries. In France, in Austria, and in Mexico, it has been painted with peasant floral patterns. So, if you have this chair in your home with furniture of other periods, it seems permissible to use a little poetic license and paint it if you like. The stencil-design included here is a

hundred years younger than the original chair.

One point to consider in decorating this simple chair is that it is hardly appropriate to give it the rather formal treatment of black background and gold stenciling. Rather, paint it in light or dark colors and transfer the design by the oil-stencil technique described in the preceding Camellia Design. You will in this way keep the chair in its proper bracket of informality.

PLATE 33. Cohasset Colonial chair. See Pattern 14.

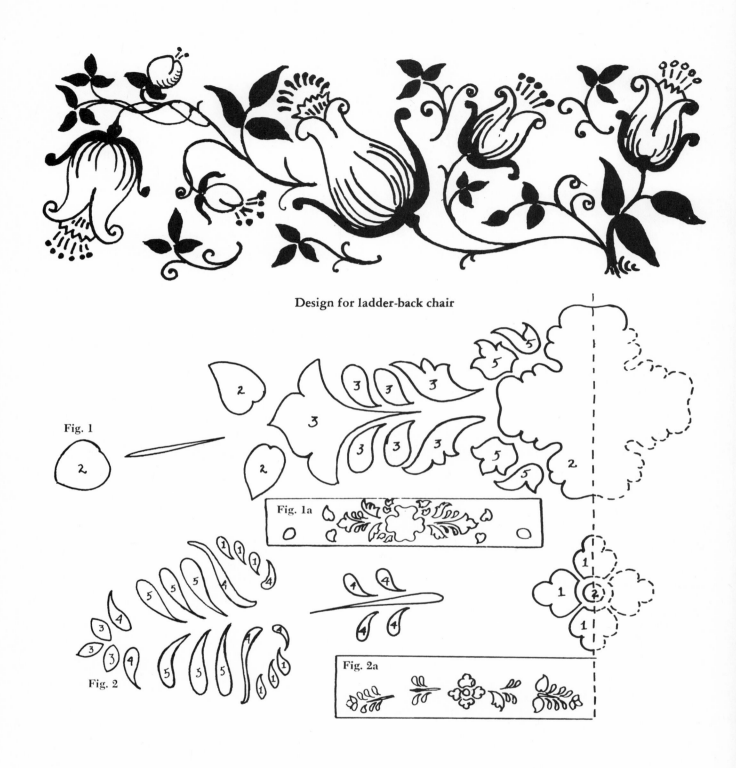

Design for ladder-back chair

Fig. 1

Fig. 1a

Fig. 2

Fig. 2a

PATTERN 14. LADDER-BACK CHAIR (*See Plate* 33)

Fig. 1: One-half of stencil pattern for each slat. *Fig. 1a:* Complete design in miniature. *Fig. 2:* One-half of over-stencil for each slat. *Fig. 2a:* Complete over-stencil design in miniature.

Ladder-Back Chair

STEP-BY-STEP DIRECTIONS
BACKGROUND

Refer to Chapter 2, Preparing Chairs for Decorating. Choose a background color and prepare chair according to instructions. (See Plate 33.)

MATERIALS

Refer to Pattern 13 and provide yourself with identical materials.

CUTTING THE STENCIL

1. Refer to Pattern 13 for oil-stencil technique.
2. Trace half the pattern (Fig. 1.) Fold tracing on dotted line and complete other side of design by tracing in reverse. In the same manner, complete tracing of Fig. 2. The completed tracings should look like sketches Fig. 1a and Fig. 2a.
3. Transfer tracings to heavy yellow oiled tracing paper and cut the stencils.

COLORS

Mix 5 small batches of paint, using spar-varnish as medium. Paint mixture should be thick, not thin.

1. *Light pink:* Add very small amounts of alizarin, cadmium red, and yellow (just a speck) to white, using varnish to moisten.
2. *Dark rose:* Mix alizarin, cadmium red, and small amount of black in varnish. Add a bit of white until desired shade of dark rose is achieved.
3. *Light green:* Mix chrome green, white, and small amount of yellow in varnish.
4. *Dark green:* Mix permanent green and black with small amount of yellow. Add a bit of white

if color seems too dark.
5. *Blue-gray:* Mix blue with a small amount of alizarin and yellow ochre. Lighten to a satisfactory tone with white.

STENCILING THE PATTERN

1. Place Fig. 1 in center of slat and anchor with thumbtacks.
2. Dip brush in paint and, holding brush in a vertical position, tap paint over open sections of stencil. Bristles of brush should meet open holes of stencil in vertical position.
3. Follow the numbers in Pattern 14 for colors—1. is light pink; 2. dark rose; 3. light green; 4. dark green 5. blue-gray.
4. Stencil Fig. 1 by tapping brush firmly over holes in pattern and following letters in Pattern 14. Allow to dry for 24 hours.
5. Place Fig. 2 in position over Fig. 1, and stencil using colors according to numbers on Pattern 14.
6. Repeat design on all four slats of chair. See Plate 33.

STRIPING

1. Refer to Chapter 4, section on Striping. Blue-gray is recommended as a striping color for this chair.
2. Mark guide-lines with chalk directly on chair where striping should appear. See Plate 33.
3. Apply striping according to step-by-step directions.

FINISHING

Refer to Chapter 3, section on Final Finishing, and follow step-by-step directions.

PLATE 34. Fine chair of American Directory style, probably made by Duncan Phyfe. A chair of similar design may be appropriately decorated with Classic motifs in Patterns 15 and 16.

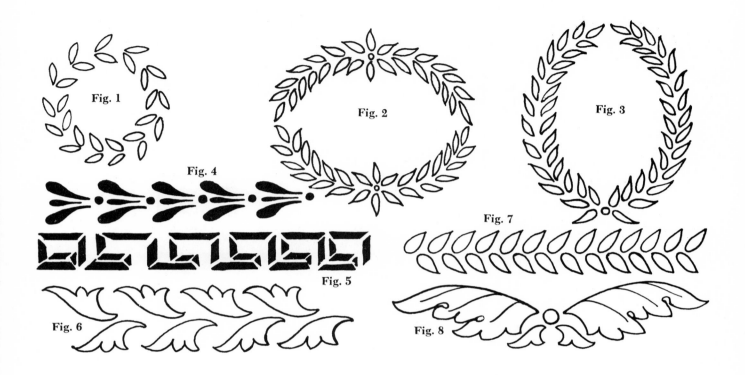

PATTERN 15. MISCELLANEOUS CLASSICAL MOTIFS

Fig. 1: Circle motif; may be used as repeat pattern for border. *Fig. 2:* Closed classic wreath motif. *Fig. 3:* Open classic wreath motif. *Figs. 4, 5, 6* and *7:* Border patterns. *Fig. 8:* Double acanthus motif.

PLATE 35. Miscellaneous stencils. Cutting and Morrow Collection.
Courtesy Metropolitan Museum of Art, New York City.

[122]

Palmette

Lyre

Leaf and Scroll

Greek Key

Acanthus

Fruit and Flower Basket

PATTERN 16.   MORE CLASSICAL MOTIFS AND A FRUIT AND FLOWER BASKET

To pull together miscellaneous pieces of furniture, there is nothing better than a classic motif. Motifs may be combined or used singly in many different settings. The background color could be black; the decoration could be a leaf border in gold with perhaps a wreath, palmette, or lyre in the center. Pattern 15 also contains several of these units.

[123]

Index